The History of God Speaking

And What God Is Saying Today

πολυμερως και πολυτροπως παλαι ο θεος λαλησας
τοις πατρασιν εν τοις προφηταις επ εσχατου των
ημερων τουτων ελαλησεν ημιν εν υιω ον εθηκεν
κληρονομον παντων δι ου και εποιησεν τους αιωνας

—ΠΡΟΣ ΕΒΡΑΙΟΥΣ 1:1–2

Les Martin

ISBN 978-1-0980-9098-2 (paperback)
ISBN 978-1-0980-9099-9 (digital)

Christian Faith Publishing, Inc.
832 Park Avenue
Meadville, PA 16335
www.christianfaithpublishing.com

All of the quotations from the scriptures are from the English Standard Version of the Bible, copyright 2007 by Crossway Bibles, a publishing ministry of Good News Publishers.

Printed in the United States of America

CONTENTS

THE HISTORY OF GOD SPEAKING

What the Scriptures Say about God Speaking Today

> Long ago, at many times and in many ways, God spoke to our fathers by the prophets, but in these last days he has spoken to us by his Son, whom he appointed the heir of all things, through whom also he created the world. (Heb. 1:1–2)

INTRODUCTION

It is nothing short of amazing to think that the God of all creation, who rules over all, would communicate to us. As the author of Hebrews makes clear, that communication came in various ways, culminating in the person of His Son. Not only did God communicate, but He left us with a record of that communication in the form of a written document—sixty-six individual books cohesively wed together as a unity that declares to us who God is and what He has done and what He will do. So complete is this revelation that we need nothing else for life and godliness! When we open the sacred text, He speaks. Why would we need any further revelation from Him? Apparently, many in the church think that we do.

The issue of God speaking personal messages outside of the recorded scriptures came out in a discussion at a home Bible study several years ago. As the discussion intensified, I made the claim that if I ever wrote a book, it would be "A History of God Speaking," making a case for God's completed revelation. One Bible study participant disagreed with me, saying that to believe God does not speak outside of His Word would limit God's ability to communicate and would dishonor the testimonies of thousands of believers who were convinced they had the experience of hearing God's voice outside of Scripture.

A few weeks later, that Bible study participant sent me a copy of a weekly devotional ministry from a well-known Pentecostal preacher who was explaining the importance of hearing fresh revelation from God. The person who sent me the devotional challenged me to be sure to put that in my book. Does God speak outside of His Word? Is there scriptural instruction in the Bible for recognizing God's voice outside of His written revelation? If we examine the written biblical history of God speaking, will that shed any light on the question?

Most evangelicals affirm that God is not silent; He speaks. But how and when and in what way does God speak? How we define speech and how we answer that question has far-reaching implications. The answer must be found in a place of certain authority. We can review the testimonies of people both past and present, whose experiences will give answers, but to claim that God was speaking is not verifiable based on human testimony alone. If we examine the Scripture, which internally claims to be the inerrant Word of God, and externally has been demonstrated to be so, we should be able to answer that question with some certainty—at least with less speculation and doubt.

In the beginning, God spoke His creation into existence. No human was listening, for none existed. After Adam and Eve were created, God appears to have spoken directly to them. Scripture also records the Lord's words to Cain and to Noah and to Abram (Abraham) and other patriarchs, including Moses and Joshua. The method of His communication was not always made clear (audible voice, vision, dream, etc.), but those communications, in whatever form they came, were recorded in the sacred text. The high priest was at times able to "hear from God" with what the Bible identifies as "Urim and Thummim" (Exod. 28:30, Lev. 8:8, Deut. 33:8, 1 Sam. 14:41, Ezek. 2:63, and Neh. 7:65)—another of the "many ways" God spoke.

The judges and the prophets seemed to be the spokespersons for God after the people of Israel arrived and settled into the land promised to them. There is evidence that God spoke to the kings as well. But how did He speak? Sometimes we are specifically told that He spoke through the "Angel of the Lord" (as with Manoah) or in a dream (as in the case of Joseph) or in a vision (as in the case of Daniel; note also: "And he said, 'Hear my words: If there is a prophet among you, I the LORD make myself known to him in a vision; I speak with him in a dream'" [Num. 12:6]). But when the Bible does not reveal the form of the communication, how did God speak? Was He heard in an audible voice? Was His communication through mental impression? And if so, how did those who believed they were receiving revelation from God know for certain that it was God speaking? To mischaracterize or misrepresent God carried severe repercussions. If a prophet of God declared he had a prophecy from God that turned out to be false, he was to be put to death (Deut. 13:1–5; 18:20–22).

The New Testament begins with the introduction of the Son of God incarnate. Jesus spoke to His generation during His three-year ministry, and He spoke directly to His disciples even after His resurrection, prior to His ascension. He spoke words recorded in the form of letters to seven congregations which appear in John's account of the Revelation. After Jesus, God's Son, ascended into heaven, these words of God were recorded and added to the already canonized OT. These included not only the four Gospel accounts of Jesus's earthly life and ministry but also messages from some of the disciples of the Lord Jesus who walked with Him during His incarnation and, several years later, to the apostle Paul.

It is not the scope of this study to argue the canon of Scripture. We begin with the premise that the sixty-six books of the Bible (thirty-nine OT books and twenty-seven NT books) constitute the Scripture—which is the Word of God. These sixty-six books make up the recorded history of God speaking, but is there more? Is God continuing to speak, and if so, how? Does He speak through the Scriptures alone, or is He giving fresh revelations? And if so, what do we do with these revelations? Do we add them to the pages of Scripture? Are these new revelations inerrant as we believe the written text to be? Do they carry the same authority? These are questions that need to be answered. Before we speculate on the nature of the testimonies of others who believe God continues to speak and who believe what they have received is true and authoritative, we need to study what we have been given in the pages of the sacred text.

The content of this book began to take shape as a result of a Bible study discussion group that met together over several weeks. I had suggested that at some point the material covered in the study would hopefully be compiled into a book. The participants' input would certainly be considered and possibly included. With tongue in cheek, one of the Bible study participants asked, "So did God tell you to write the book?" His book is already written and needs no further revelation to make it complete.

The Wonder of God's Revelation
in Various Ways in the Past

As we consider the OT, Moses penned the first five books of the Bible more than one thousand four hundred years before the incarnation of Jesus. The entire content of Genesis occurred before Moses was born. There were other authors including prophets and kings, shepherds and priests, and statesmen and farmers. Various people made contributions bit by bit, but no prophet or prophecy delivered all of Scripture. As wonderful as it was, it remained incomplete. These writings included history and biography and poetry and prophecy. There were legal documents and personal testimonies—all of them revealing the wonder of God and the desperate condition of man. Again, the OT was a literary masterpiece—an ancient as well as a modern marvel—but still incomplete.

Consider also how this revelation came. It was not just the musings of men but actually the words of God, even though His words were communicated through human agency and literary forms. Sometimes God spoke directly. Sometimes His revelation came indirectly through dreams. At other times, His will and purpose were made known through circumstances, through miraculous events, and through the prophecies of prophets and kings. There were illustrations and parables and fables and riddles, and chronicles of the kings and angel conversations and even direct audible words from God Himself. Once God even made His purposes known to a compromising prophet through the words being spoken by a donkey! As incredible and amazing and varied as all of this was, it still was incomplete. The completion of the revelation of God was yet to come.

The author of Hebrews declares that *God spoke to our fathers by the prophets.* Though it was through the prophets that the fathers heard God, God says that He spoke to the fathers. In other words, though they received God's Word through the prophets, this was to be considered as God speaking to them. When the fathers heard and understood the message of the prophets, they were hearing God speak! When we hear and understand the Word, the Scriptures, we are hearing God speak! His written Word is equivalent to His spoken Word. When we read the text of Scripture, we are hearing His voice! He is speaking. God has used various instruments to speak to the fathers and to believers throughout the centuries, but it is still God speaking!

God raised up prophets, and He gave them His word so that they could make it known to the people. The prophets were God's spokespersons. God could have chosen any number of ways to make His word known. He could have written His message in the sky, perhaps much like the message to Belshazzar that was written on the wall in the book of Daniel. He could have spoken from the mountain for all to hear, much like He communicated to Moses in the OT; or to Peter, James, and John on the Mount of Transfiguration, recorded in the Gospels. He could have chosen to whisper His revelation into the heart of every Israelite, but He did not do that either. He spoke to the prophets, and they, in turn, thundered to the others, "Thus says the Lord!" The prophets were the mouthpieces of God. What they said was what God was speaking. For a prophet to declare, "Hear the Word of the Lord," was to inform the people that what was being communicated was what God was saying. The prophets were the delivery system, the speakers, if you will, but what was heard was from God. Unfortunately, the people listened to the prophets about as well as people listen to the written Word.

God used various literary forms to reveal Himself, which included historical narrative, biography, poetry, parables, prophecy, and allegory. He has spoken. He has not been silent. The revelation of God

> came piecemeal, bit by bit. Various persons made
> their contributions; no one prophet or prophecy

delivered it all. Abraham was the recipient of some basic revelation. David received some more. Isaiah, Jeremiah, Ezekiel and Daniel provided still more as God revealed His truth to them... These... descriptions are by no means to be understood as a disparagement of Old Testament revelation, as though it were unworthy. The many fragments and varied ways point to the graciousness and versatility of God in matching His revelation to the capability of men to understand it.[1]

But the final completed revelation was yet to come in the person of the Son of God Himself!

As wonder-filled as the OT is and as amazing as the manner in which this revelation was given, something superior had arrived. Jesus Christ, God the Son, has now appeared, and He has spoken. The NT is the story of the Son who has spoken—whose revelation of Himself is now complete. What we have is all we need for life and godliness. Consider that the Gospels are the revelation of Jesus Christ who came to earth. The Acts of the Apostles is the record of His ascension into heaven and the establishment of His church on earth. The epistles are the record of His work in the building of His body, the church. The Revelation is about His coming in power and great glory as He brings His plan and purpose to the ultimate conclusion.

Though the OT stands alone, with the revelation of the NT, the revelation of the Son, God's person and purpose became increasingly clear.

> The Old Testament tells us in at least two places (Jer. 23:18 and Amos 3:7) that the prophets were let in on the secrets of God. Yet at times they wrote the secrets without understanding them (1 Peter 1:10–11). In Jesus Christ they are both fulfilled

---

[1.] Homer A. Kent Jr., *The Epistle to the Hebrews: A Commentary* (Winona Lake, Indiana: BMH Books, 1972), 33–34.

and understood. He is God's final word. "For as many as may be the promises of God, in Him, they are yes; wherefore also by Him is our Amen to the glory of God through us" (2 Cor. 1:20). Every promise of God resolves itself in Christ. All the promises become yes—verified and fulfilled. Jesus Christ is the supreme and the final revelation.[2]

He has spoken! And His revelation is complete, and nothing more needs to be said. In these recent days, He has spoken to us by His Son! Can you believe it? He has come! He has spoken! The living Word has made Himself known! He is the speaking Son of God! He has made known His will and His purpose. "These last days," as the author of Hebrews used the term, began with the coming of the Lord Jesus into the world. Therefore, we have been living in "these last days," the last days of history before the complete and final establishment of the kingdom of God. These are the last days because the decisive battle has already been fought and won. Christ has triumphed over sin and death and hell by His cross. We wait eagerly for the consummation of His kingdom. The fact that these are the last days tells us that the words God has spoken here, through His Son in the NT, are decisive words, final words. These words will not be followed by any other words. They will not be replaced or superseded by any additional words. What are these words that are the final words, the words that have been spoken by God in these last days? They are words spoken to us by His Son.

The word God has spoken in these last days is the revelation of His Son, which includes the person of Jesus, the teachings of Jesus, and the commentaries on the teachings of Jesus as given to us in the pages of the New Testament. I appreciate the candor of John Piper who said,

When I complain that I don't hear the word of God when I feel a desire to hear the voice of

---

[2.] John MacArthur, *Hebrews* (Chicago: Moody Press, 1983), 8.

God, and get frustrated that he does not speak in ways that I may crave, what am I really saying? Am I really saying that I have exhausted this final decisive Word revealed to me so fully in the New Testament? Have I really exhausted this word? Has it become so much a part of me that it has shaped my very being and given me life and guidance? Or have I treated it lightly—skimmed it like a newspaper, dipped in like a taste-tester— and then decided I wanted something different, something more? This is what I fear I am guilty of more than I wish to admit. God is calling us to hear his final decisive Word—to meditate on it and study it and memorize it and linger over it and soak in it until it saturates us to the center of our being.[3]

The Son of God was not just a prophet, though many believe that was all Jesus was. He was and is "the radiance of the glory of God and the exact imprint of his nature." He is superior to the prophets in every way, and what He gave to us was the final, completed revelation of God! We must never make too little of this passage: "In these last days he has spoken to us by his Son." Jesus came in the flesh. He has spoken by coming to us. Who He was and what He said and what He accomplished is the apex and completion of God's Word to us. Additional remarks spoken by John Piper are in order here.

Every time I begin to complain that God is silent and that I need God to speak to me—at that moment I should stop and ask: Have I heard this Word? Is this Word from God—spoken in the Son of God—so short and simple that I have finished with it and now I need more—another

---

[3.] John Piper, Desiring God, from the manuscript of a sermon, *In These Last Days, God Has Spoken by His Son* March 31, 1996, p. 6.

word? Have I really heard the Word of God in person and the teaching and the work of the Son? Is the aching of my soul and the confusion of my mind really owing to the fact that I have exhausted hearing this Word and need another word? And so, I feel another gracious rebuke to my unperceptive and presumptuous ears.[4]

God has spoken to us by His Son!

In these last days, God still speaks. How does He speak? God speaks through the revelation of the Son as heir of all things. The fact that the author of Hebrews included this must mean that God wanted us to know that Jesus, the Son of God, is able to make good in the end on all of His precious promises. He can because He is the heir of all things. He made everything, and everything belongs to Him, so everything is at His disposal. Everything is subjected to Him. The One who is the heir of all things is in complete control of all things and the owner of all things. All things natural and super-natural are in His control. When He said the meek shall inherit the earth, because the earth belongs to Him, He can fulfill that promise. When Paul said that nothing could separate us from the love of God and proceeded to list everything imaginable, Jesus can make good on that promise because all of those things are in His hands. When He promised the end of tears and pain and death, those things are certain to end because He sovereignly controls everything that would bring on such responses. The prophets were the mouthpieces of God. Jesus is God. In the past, God spoke through the prophets. In these last days, He has spoken through His own Son—the Son who is the heir of all things.

God has spoken to us through the revelation of the Son who is superior to all things.

The epistle to the Hebrews was written to declare the fact that Jesus is superior to everything. He is greater than the angels. He is greater than Moses and the Law. He is greater than the high priests

---

4. Ibid., 4.

and the sacrificial system. He is the final and ultimate fulfillment of the law and the prophets. He is the better covenant, having fulfilled the requirements of the former covenant. He is a better high priest without beginning or end. His sacrifice was a once-for-all sacrifice, complete, never to be repeated. It provided not mere covering for sin but actual atonement, propitiation, satisfaction coming from the Father that the price for sin had been paid in full.

It is this One, who is superior to all things, who has spoken in these last days. God has graciously recorded His words in a book. This is no ordinary book. It is a living book, not that it is growing in content or changing in meaning, but it is living in that it is the voice of God to those who belong to Jesus through His atoning sacrifice. The question has been asked, why did God reveal Himself? What was the end goal?

> The end goal of "revelation" is not the perpetual experience of revelation itself. Revelation instead is a means to an end. It is the way by which the eternal God makes himself known to sinful men who are hopelessly lost apart from his Son the Lord Jesus Christ. Revelation has as its end the making known of men of the one and only God, and Jesus Christ who he has sent.[5]

Read it and hear God speaking, and He makes Himself known using the method He has chosen to do so.

[5.] O. Palmer Robertson, *The Final Word* (Carlisle, PA: The Banner of Truth Trust, 1993), 52–53. This small book, particularly chapters 2 and 3, is helpful in providing a solid explanation, making the case that God's written revelation is the final record of God speaking.

In the Beginning, God Speaks

God is recorded as speaking within the Godhead calling the created world into existence. We know that Moses recorded the first five books of the Bible. It was necessary for this information to be communicated, either through "tradition" passed down by Adam through successive generations, guarded by the Holy Spirit (2 Pet. 1), or by direct revelation from God to Moses as Moses penned the Law, including the Genesis creation account. How Moses received this revelation, we are not specifically told, but Jesus affirmed the divine authorship and accuracy of the OT Law and affirmed its authenticity as the very Word of God recorded by Moses (see Mark 12:26 and Luke 24:44 as examples).

In regard to creation, at least ten times in the first chapter of Genesis, we are told that "God said" (vv. 3, 6, 9, 11, 14, 20, 24, 26, 28, 29). Three times we are told that "God called" (vv. 5, 8, 10). Verse 22 says that "God blessed them, saying…," and verse 28 also says, "God blessed them." In Genesis 2:3, "God blessed the seventh day and made it holy." In verse 18, "God said, 'It is not good that the man should be alone.'" This conversation was within the triune Godhead indicated in the text by the statement concerning the intention to create man—"Let *us* make man in *our* image, after *our* likeness." We have been allowed to listen to the record of that conversation.

God apparently spoke directly, to Adam and Eve in Genesis 1:28, after having created them, pronouncing His blessing on them. He commanded them to "be fruitful and multiply and fill the earth and subdue it, and have dominion." Continuing to speak, God explained to His human creation the source of their food (1:29–30). The information was repeated (2:16) along with an additional statement prohibiting them from eating from the tree of the knowledge of good and evil. God warned that the penalty of death would immediately follow if the prohibition was breached.

It is clear from the first two chapters of Genesis that God was the Creator and the sustainer of His creation. He communicated that He was the ultimate judge, holding the power of life and death. God made known His will in regard to the population of the earth. The form of God's communication to them is not clear, though, in relation to the language in chapter 3, it seems reasonable to assume that God, in some visible form, communicated "face-to-face."

For the most part, God chose to withhold from us revelation concerning the fall of Satan and his angels. Satan appeared suddenly before Adam and Eve and began a subtle attack in regard to God's revelation to them—"Did God actually say…?" Doubt was successfully planted in Eve's mind regarding the content of God's word. Satan, in the form of a serpent, moved from asking a question to completely denying God's revelation. God's promise to the couple that if they disobeyed, they would surely die, became assurance from Satan that nothing of the sort would happen, "You will not surely die." The enemy continued to distort the revelation of God with a faulty assumption and interpretation of what God had said as well as a direct challenge to the motivation of God's revelation. It is interesting that it was in regard to a misappropriation of God's word that led to the first sin.

As God called for them, Adam and Eve hid from their Creator. When Adam finally did answer, he revealed some of the immediate results of sin, which included fear of God, a self-consciousness that had not been present before, and personal shame. Adam was forced to face his sin with God's question, "Have you eaten of the tree of which I commanded you not to eat." Though both Adam and Eve offered excuses, Adam directly blamed Eve for giving him the fruit and indirectly blamed God for having given the woman to him in the first place! Adam did, however, admit to breaking God's command.

Turning to the woman, God asked her for an explanation: "What is this that you have done?" God's words established the guilt. She pled ignorance, blaming the serpent for deceiving her. The scriptures do affirm that Eve was deceived (1 Tim. 2:14), but there was no question or confusion concerning what God had actually said.

God continued to speak (vv. 14–19), pronouncing judgments on the serpent, and the one behind the serpent, Satan, on the woman, on the man, and on the entire created universe. Against the backdrop of God's judgments, a promise of mercy and grace was given in the enigmatic prophecy of an offspring that would ultimately crush the head of the serpent (v. 15). Mercy was demonstrated in the garments of skin given to clothe the nakedness of the sinful couple. In this act of mercy was a hint that any covering of sin would require the shedding of blood. The fulfillment of the promise of death as judgment immediately was demonstrated.

Once again, we have a record of a conversation within the Godhead (3:22–24). The consequences of sin were mentioned as humans were separated from God and from the tree of life. Verse 22 suggests that God did not unilaterally condemn all to an eternal separation from Him, but, as an act of mercy, the first humans were prevented from eating from the tree of life after they sinned, which presumably would have locked in condemnation for all humans that would follow, without any possible redemption, a redemption which had been enigmatically promised in Genesis 3:15.

It is reasonable to assume that God communicated to Adam His requirements for the offerings that were to be presented to Him, as well as requirements for those who would offer them. It is in relation to offerings and sacrifices that we are introduced to Adam and Eve's offspring. "And the Lord had regard for Abel and his offering, but for Cain and his offering he had no regard" (Gen. 4:4–5). The rejection of Cain's offering probably involved more than just what was offered, though that may have been a factor. God counseled Cain (v. 6), but no response was recorded. Instead Cain talked to his brother and then killed him. The Lord spoke to Cain again (vv. 9, 10–12) pronouncing judgment on him, effectively ending Cain's farming career. He became a fugitive and a wanderer. Cain complained that his punishment was too great to endure. Having been driven "from the face of God" was seen by Cain as a death sentence—"whoever finds me will kill me." God spoke again, promising Cain that this would not happen and gave Cain a mark to somehow protect him from anyone who might seek to kill him. "Cain went away from the presence of the Lord." How the Lord communicated to Cain is not revealed. It is inconclusive to draw inference from the phrase, "the presence of the Lord."

In Genesis 5, we are introduced to Enoch. There is no record in the Pentateuch of God speaking to him; however, the record of Enoch as a prophet of God speaking a prophecy regarding the return of the Lord in great power to judge the ungodly does appear in the epistle of Jude.

> It was also about these that Enoch, the seventh from Adam, prophesied, saying, "Behold, the Lord comes with ten thousands of his holy ones, to execute judgment on all and to convict all the ungodly of all their deeds of ungodliness that they have committed in such an ungodly way, and of all the harsh things that ungodly sinners have spoken against him." (Jude 1:14–15)

This was the first prophetic message spoken by God to a prophet, who would then announce the prophecy to others. The author of Hebrews (11:5) provides additional details; Enoch did not see death, and he was commended prior to being taken, as having pleased God. Though not stated, it can be assumed that the commendation came from God Himself.

Though still early in human history, mankind was entrenched in sin. In Genesis 6, God declared His message of destruction as well as protection (6:3, 7, 13–21). We have another example of a Trinitarian conversation, this time as a promise that had a specified measurement of time attached. Verse 7 communicated God's intention to "blot out man whom I have created from the face of the land…for I am sorry that I have made them." God revealed to Noah

His intentions of judgment and the reason for those intentions, as well as specific instructions for Noah and his family to be rescued from destruction.

God declared the establishment of His covenant with Noah (6:18). Further information about the ark, Noah's family, the animals, and food for all on the ark were given. The method of revelation is not stated, but there was no question that this was from the Lord. Noah's obedience in building the ark according to instructions received was summarized in one verse, "Noah did this; he did all that God commanded him" (6:22). God spoke specifically of the clean animals of which Noah was to take "seven pairs...the male and his mate" of each (7:2), and single pairs of all unclean animals ("the male and his mate"). Once again, "Noah did all that the Lord had commanded him" (7:5). Noah's actions of sending out a raven and a dove as the flood subsided were not credited as a revelation from God. These may have been Noah's independent actions apart from God's instructions.

In Genesis 8:15 and following, God again spoke to Noah telling him to disembark with his family, along with the animals, and Noah obeyed God's word. In response to the sacrifices that Noah made to God, Moses wrote,

> And when the LORD smelled the pleasing aroma, the LORD said in his heart, "I will never again curse the ground because of man, for the intention of man's heart is evil from his youth. Neither will I ever again strike down every living creature as I have done. While the earth remains, seedtime and harvest, cold and heat, summer and winter, day and night, shall not cease." (8:21–22)

This promise from God may have been revealed directly to Moses as he recorded the Law. There is no clear indication that God revealed to Noah what "the Lord said in his heart" in regard to His promise to never again curse the ground. In the next chapter, as God spoke the content of the covenant He made with Noah (9:9 ff.), some of what He had said in His heart was included.

How God spoke to Noah we do not know. Was this "face-to-face" in some way or an audible voice? Was this somehow spoken to Noah into his heart or mind? Does the text itself give any clues to the answer? God first called Noah and his sons to "be fruitful and multiply and fill the earth" (9:1). God announced the dread of the animal kingdom toward man. Along with green plants, God gave permission to man to eat meat, but not the blood. God then gave a command in relation to the shedding of blood. This was followed by the repeated command to be fruitful and multiply. Then came the revelation of a covenant with Noah and his sons and "with every living creature that is with you." There was no further record of God speaking to Noah.

In Genesis 11, the people decided to organize a world religion and build a tower as a place to rally together. It was the people's determination to build a tower "to make a name for themselves." The divine response to this determination was a conversation recorded among the Godhead,

> And the LORD came down to see the city and the tower, which the children of man had built. And the LORD said, "Behold, they are one people, and they have all one language, and this is only the beginning of what they will do. And nothing that they propose to do will now be impossible for them. Come, let us go down and there confuse their language, so that they may not understand one another's speech." (11:5–7).

Moses received this conversation from the Lord and recorded what was said, which no human heard. There is no indication that the people understood this confusion of language to be a judgment from God, nor that their scattering was God's doing. "So the LORD dispersed them from there over the face of all the earth, and they left off building the city" (v. 8). We only know this because God revealed it to Moses.

Before we move into the narrative sections of Genesis to observe God speaking to Abraham and Isaac and Jacob and Joseph, we should consider God speaking in relation to Job. The book of Job opens with an introduction to the man and then moves the reader to a place where "the sons of God came to present themselves before the Lord, and Satan also came among them." The Lord spoke directly to Satan, "From where have you come? ...Have you considered my servant Job" (1:7). Satan answered the Lord, and the Lord permitted Satan to inflict Job's family and to destroy Job's possessions but was not permitted to touch Job. In Job 2, the sons of God (angels) again came to present themselves to the Lord, and Satan was again present. God asked the same question of Satan, "Have you considered my servant Job?" Satan challenged God that if he was allowed to bring bodily harm to Job, Job would curse God. Permission was granted to inflict suffering, but Satan was commanded to spare Job's life. When God spoke to the angels, it appears to have been face-to-face.

The counsel from Job's friends and Job's replies to that counsel occupy most of the book. In the context of these rebukes and rebuttals, several revelations about God were spoken. When and where and to whom these statements were originally revealed is not made known. One amazing example is in Job 19:23–27.

> Oh that my words were written! Oh that they were inscribed in a book! Oh that with an iron pen and lead they were engraved in the rock forever! For I know that my Redeemer lives, and at the last he will stand upon the earth. And after my skin has been thus destroyed, yet in my flesh I shall see God, whom I shall see for myself, and my eyes shall behold, and not another. My heart faints within me!

Two observations are in order. First, Job was not aware that what he was enduring and what He was saying would be in a book of divine revelation. Second, Job had a very clear and detailed awareness of redemption, resurrection, and glorification that is not found anywhere in the OT prior to the time of Job. Whether he knew it or not, Job seemed to be speaking revelatory words, words from God that would much later be articulated in Scripture in passages such as 1 Corinthians 15.

Following the words of rebuke and the rebuttals by Job, recorded in chapters 3–37, God spoke to Job "out of a whirlwind" (38:1). God asked Job a series of questions in a lengthy dissertation (Job 38:2–39:30), and then called on Job for an answer, "The Lord said to Job, 'Shall a faultfinder contend with the Almighty? He who argues with God, let him answer it'" (40:1–2). A second time the Lord called to Job out of a whirlwind, "Dress for action like a man; I will question you, and you make it known to me" (40:7). The Lord continued this discourse through the end of chapter 41.

God then turned His attention to one of Job's friends, Eliphaz. He represented not only himself but also the other two friends. Eliphaz was rebuked, corrected, and told to go to Job and

> offer up a burnt offering for yourselves. And my servant Job shall pray for you; for I will accept his prayer not to deal with you according to your folly. For you have not spoken of me what is right as my servant Job has. (42:8)

No further words from God to Job or the friends were recorded. God's revelation to Job seems to be His voice rather than some physical appearance.

3

God Speaks to Abraham, Isaac, Jacob, and Joseph

Abram (Abraham) was a pagan worshipper, but God spoke to him with a command and a promised blessing, and Abram obeyed. It appears that God's initial speaking to Abram was either a voice or some internal communication into Abram's mind or heart (Gen. 12:7). However, there is little evidence that God communicated through the minds of various individuals what He wanted them to know. That may have been the case, but there is no clear affirmation for this kind of communication in the Genesis account.

In some form, God appeared to Abram and promised to give to his descendants the land through which Abram had passed. Abram built an altar to the Lord and "called upon his name." He then continued his journey. In Egypt, Abram lied about his relationship with his wife, Sarai, intending to protect himself from potential harm or death. God afflicted Pharaoh and his household with "great plagues" (12:17). The text does not indicate that the truth about Sarai was revealed to Pharaoh, but rather the sudden judgments caused Pharaoh to question Abram. God intervened but did not speak.

Following the separation of Abram and Lot (chapter 13), the Lord spoke to Abram and showed him the land that had been spoken of earlier in Genesis 12. God said of this land, "I will give to you and your offspring forever" (13:15). Abram was promised offspring "as the dust of the earth" (13:16) and told to walk through the land. We are not given the details of the means of this transmission of information, only that "the Lord said to Abram" (13:14). After Abram delivered Lot from a coalition of kings and their militias, he was met by a king-priest, Melchizedek. A prophecy spoken by Melchizedek, which apparently had come from God, was given to Abram.

> And he blessed him and said, "Blessed be Abram by God Most High, Possessor of heaven and earth; and blessed be God Most High, who has delivered your enemies into your hand!" (14:19–20)

No further information was provided.

In Genesis 15, God's affirmation of His covenant with Abram is recorded. This time, revelation was identified as "the word of the Lord" coming in the form of a vision. This vision, however, was interactive in that Abram asked for confirmation of God's promise to give the land to him and his descendants: "How am I to know that I shall possess it?" (15:8). God called Abram to bring specific animals. No longer a vision, Abram literally brought the animals, cut the covenant pieces, and placed them in two columns. As the sun was going down, God caused a deep sleep to fall upon Abram. Presumably the vision continued as Abram was given a nightmarish revelation of a four-hundred-year servanthood for his descendants, but there was also the promise of deliverance from that oppression, and that deliverance would be accompanied by great possessions. None of this would happen in Abram's lifetime. The covenant was ratified without condition, by the Lord, as He alone passed between the pieces in the form of "a smoking firepot and a flaming torch" (15:17). God told Abram of the land that his descendants would possess (15:19–20).

In chapter 16, God introduced "the angel of the Lord,"[6] who first appeared to Hagar, the handmaid of Sarai. "The angel of the Lord

---

[6.] A brief comment regarding *the angel of the Lord* is in order. The angel of the Lord appeared in many of the passages we have considered (Gen. 16:7; Gen. 21:17; Gen. 22:11, 15; Exod. 3:1–2; Num. 22:22, 26; Judg. 13:2–3). This angel can be identified as Christ in a pre-incarnate appearance (Judg. 13:15–18 compare with Isa. 9:6, 28:29; also see Mal. 3:1 "angel [messenger] of the covenant"). As would be expected, the angel of the Lord does not appear after found her...and he said, Hagar" (16:7–8). This meeting between Hagar and "the angel of the Lord" was most likely an encounter with the pre-incarnate Second Person of the triune God, the Lord Jesus. The angel of the Lord found Hagar and talked to her, and she answered Him. He pronounced a prophetic word over her regarding her unborn offspring, Ishmael. Hagar named the place where this happened as "You are a God of seeing." She said, "Truly I have seen him who looks after me" (16:13). This was a face-to-face encounter.

In chapter 17, God spoke to Abram concerning circumcision and the covenant: "The Lord appeared to him [Abram]" (17:1). Abram fell on his face, presumably, before Him (17:1–3). This could have been a vision but appears to be more than that. Verse 22 says, "When he had finished speaking with Abraham, God went up from him." It was here that God reaffirmed His covenant with Abram and changed the name of His servant to Abraham. The covenant sign of circumcision was introduced, and specific details were given. The promise of the land was restated and affirmed to be an everlasting possession. Abraham was also told to change his wife's name to Sarah, and it was promised that Sarah would be the mother of Abraham's offspring, and the name of this offspring would be Isaac. Isaac would be born in about one year from the time of this revelation. God also told Abraham of His blessing on Ishmael.

Chapter 18 begins as did the last chapter: "And the Lord appeared to him" (18:1). However, the statement is followed by the appearance of three men standing in front of Abraham. When these three guests appeared, Lot had already separated from Abraham and moved to Sodom. From the context, one of the guests was clearly the Lord Himself; this was not only stated in verse 1 but was also revealed later as Abraham interceded for the righteous in Sodom.

---

the birth of Christ. The OT angel of the Lord demanded worship, something that would never be demanded by a holy angel of God (See Exod. 3:1–5 as compared with Rev. 19:10 and 22:8–9). Christ also appeared in the OT under the name LORD (Gen. 18:1–2, 22, 19:1; Josh. 6:2 (cf. w/ 5:13–15); Isa. 6:1–5 (cf. John 12:39–41). In relation to the Father, and in a visible presence, Jesus was the angel of Jehovah in the OT and the Son of God in the NT. When the "angel of the Lord" spoke, God was speaking.

The other two men were angels who were assigned to carry out the judgment. This had to be a face-to-face encounter. A meal was prepared, and Abraham stood with them while they ate. In verse 16, the two men (angels) got up and left, and the conversation continued between the Lord and Abraham. It seems reasonable to conclude that this was another pre-incarnate appearance of Jesus.

Chapters 20 and 21 contain two interludes regarding God speaking. God appeared to Abimelech in a dream concerning the fact that Sarah was Abraham's wife (20:3, 6). The message from God to Abimelech was, "Behold, you are a dead man because of the woman whom you have taken, for she is a man's wife." In the dream, Abimelech argued for his innocence, and God responded.

> Yes, I know that you have done this in the integrity of your heart, and it was I who kept you from sinning against me. Therefore, I did not let you touch her. Now then, return the man's wife, for he is a prophet, so that he will pray for you, and you shall live. But if you do not return her, know that you shall surely die, you and all who are yours. (vv. 6–7)

God spoke to a pagan king through a dream in order to protect Abraham and Sarah. Note that God referred to Abraham as "a prophet."

The second interlude in chapter 21 involved the conflict between Sarah and Hagar. As Sarah called for the casting out of Hagar and Ishmael, God spoke to Abraham, affirming the decision to do what Sarah demanded, reminding Abraham that Isaac, not Ishmael, was the son of promise. Abraham obeyed. He gave Hagar bread and a skin of water and sent her and her son away. With an empty waterskin and little hope for survival, Hagar wept, and God heard her. The angel of God "called to Hagar from heaven" (v. 17). This must have been an audible voice. God declared that He had heard her voice, and He opened Hagar's eyes to see a well of water.

Chapter 22 continued the revelation of God's test for Abraham in regard to his son Isaac, calling Abraham to sacrifice his son (22:1–2). God spoke and Abraham answered, "Here am I." The message calling for the sacrifice of Abraham's son seems to have been an audible voice from God. As Abraham was about to plunge the knife into his son, the angel of the Lord spoke from heaven (v. 11), in what also seems to have been an audible voice. God called out his name, and Abraham answered again, "Here I am." Abraham was instructed not to lay a hand on his son, "for now I know that you fear God, seeing you have not withheld your son, your only son from me" (22:12). A second time, in verse 15 ff., the angel of the Lord spoke from heaven. Since Abraham had not withheld his son, God reaffirmed His blessing.

> I will surely bless you, and I will surely multiply your offspring as the stars of heaven and as the sand that is on the seashore. And your offspring shall possess the gate of his enemies, and in your offspring shall all the nations of the earth be blessed, because you have obeyed my voice. (vv. 17–18)

When the angel of the Lord spoke, generally it was a face-to-face encounter involving a pre-incarnate appearance of Jesus Christ. Here the angel of the Lord was not seen, but only His voice was heard from heaven. Notice verse 18: "Because you have obeyed *my voice*" (emphases added).

When the time came for Isaac to be married, Abraham called upon his servant to go and find a wife for his son (Gen. 24). Abraham affirmed that the Lord had taken him from his father's house, and he said to his servant who was in charge of his household that God "will send his angel before you, and you shall take a wife for my son from there" (24:7). The servant set up a series of circumstances that, if met, would point to the one who was to be the wife of Isaac—"Let her be the one whom you have appointed for your servant Isaac. By this I shall know that you have shown steadfast love to my master" (v. 14).

What the servant had requested appeared to be happening. "The man gazed at her in silence to learn whether the Lord had prospered his journey or not" (v. 21). Was this a method that should be used today to "discern the will of God"? It is important to remember that not everything in the Bible is a prescription for our imitation. God is not obligated by anything that we might attempt to arrange to discern His direction. The words of Abraham regarding God sending His angel to make the servant's objective successful may have be operative, but there is no mention of angelic intervention in the text. This may be more accurately applied to the providential workings of God.

Because Isaac's wife, Rebekah, was barren (25:22–23), Isaac prayed for Rebekah that she might bear children. God answered, and she conceived twins. Feeling the struggle within, Rebekah inquired of the Lord,

> And the LORD said to her, "Two nations are in your womb, and two peoples from within you shall be divided; the one shall be stronger than the other, the older shall serve the younger."

How the Lord communicated His word, the text does not say, except that "The Lord said…"

Because of a famine (26:2–5), Isaac traveled to Gerar, which was ruled by the Philistine king, Abimelech. The Lord appeared to Isaac with instructions not to go to Egypt. The Lord affirmed His presence with Isaac and assured him that His promises given to Abraham were passed on to him. When God physically appears in the OT, it is reasonable to conclude that these are pre-incarnate appearances of Jesus. Sadly, Isaac mimicked his father's actions by lying to the foreign king, claiming his wife to be his sister. There is no record of a divine warning to the king here. Instead, Abimelech saw Isaac with Rebekah and concluded that this was definitely not his sister! Following a skirmish over some wells that had been dug, Isaac traveled to Beersheba.

> And the Lord appeared to him that same night and said, "I am the God of Abraham your father.

Fear not, for I am with you and will bless you and
multiply your offspring for my servant Abraham's
sake." (26:24)

This could have been a vision or another pre-incarnate visit.
There was no further revelation to Isaac recorded.

The next record of God speaking was to Jacob (28:12 ff.),
which began as a dream while Jacob was sleeping. Jacob saw a ladder
between heaven and earth with the angels of God ascending and
descending. He heard the Lord speak.

I am the LORD, the God of Abraham your father
and the God of Isaac. The land on which you
lie I will give to you and to your offspring. Your
offspring shall be like the dust of the earth, and
you shall spread abroad to the west and to the
east and to the north and to the south, and in
you and your offspring shall all the families of
the earth be blessed. Behold, I am with you and
will keep you wherever you go and will bring you
back to this land. For I will not leave you until I
have done what I have promised you. (28:13–15)

With that, Jacob awoke.

God instructed Jacob to return to the land of his fathers and was
given the promise that He would be with him (31:3). Jacob secretly
left with his family and all their possessions. Laban pursued Jacob
and in three days caught up with the caravan. Laban reminded Jacob
that it was in his power to do him harm, but God had appeared to
him in a dream and warned him not to say anything good or bad to
Jacob (31:29). Laban did not indicate God's method of communication, but the message was clear to him. This revelation is interesting
because it was within the context of Laban trying to rescue his gods
that had been secretly taken by Rachel! Jacob interpreted the divine
revelation to Laban in this way: "God saw my affliction and the labor
of my hands and rebuked you last night" (31:42).

"Jacob went on his way and the angels of God met him" (Gen. 32:1). There is nothing here to help us to identify the form of this message from God. This is reminiscent of 28:17. As Jacob prepared to meet his brother Esau, he sent his wives and children and servants ahead and was left alone. It was here that

> a man wrestled with him until the breaking of the day. Then he said, "Let me go, for the day has broken." But Jacob said, "I will not let you go unless you bless me." And he said to him, "What is your name?" And he said, "Jacob." Then he said, "Your name shall no longer be called Jacob, but Israel, for you have striven with God and with men, and have prevailed." Then Jacob asked him, "Please tell me your name." But he said, "Why is it that you ask my name?" And there he blessed him. So Jacob called the name of the place Peniel, saying, "For I have seen God face to face, and yet my life has been delivered." (28:25–30)

Notice that the "man" is identified as "God" in verse 28. Centuries later the prophet Hosea would affirm Jacob's encounter with God: "He strove with the angel and prevailed; he wept and sought his favor. He met God at Bethel and there God spoke with us" (Hos. 12:4). The God-man-angel was the pre-incarnate Jesus.

In Genesis 35:1, God commanded Jacob to go to Bethel. We are not told the method God used to command Jacob. The instructions are interesting: "Arise, go up to Bethel and dwell there. Make an altar there to the God who appeared to you when you fled from your brother Esau." Here was confirmation concerning the revelation in the dream in 28:18. This was stated again in verse 7: "And there he built an altar and called the place El-bethel, because there, God had revealed himself to him when he fled from his brother." God appeared to Jacob again.

> And God said to him, "Your name is Jacob; no longer shall your name be called Jacob, but Israel shall be your name." So he called his name Israel. And God said to him, "I am God Almighty: be fruitful and multiply. A nation and a company of nations shall come from you, and kings shall come from your own body. The land that I gave to Abraham and Isaac I will give to you, and I will give the land to your offspring after you." Then God went up from him in the place where he had spoken with him. (Gen. 35:10–13)

The statement that God "appeared" and then "went up from him" suggests that God had visited Jacob in some visible form.

Joseph and his brothers were introduced in Genesis 37. The dreams recorded here and in the next few chapters were not specifically said to be from God, but that would become evident later. Joseph's announcement of his dreams to his family regarding his position in the family set in motion the providential workings of God in his life, leading to his exalted position in Egypt and placing him in the position to preserve his family. In God's providence, Joseph was sold into slavery by his brothers. He was eventually given a position as a trusted servant to the captain of the guard. The captain's wife attempted to seduce Joseph; when he resisted, she made accusations against him, and he was imprisoned. However, the Lord was with Joseph, and he was placed in charge of the prisoners while incarcerated himself. During his incarceration, the pharaoh's cupbearer and chief baker were imprisoned because they had displeased the pharaoh. While in prison, each had a dream, which Joseph was able to accurately interpret. The interpretations were not credited as revelations from God, but that is implied in the text.

Joseph requested that the cupbearer remember that he had interpreted the dream for him, but the cupbearer soon forgot about

Joseph (40:23). Nothing happened for two years until the pharaoh had a dream that none of his wise men or magicians were able to interpret. It was then that the cupbearer remembered Joseph's intervention, and he shared it with the pharaoh. When Pharaoh summoned Joseph to interpret his dream, Joseph said, "It is not me; God will give Pharaoh a favorable answer" (41:16). Joseph explained, "God has revealed to Pharaoh what he is about to do" (41:25), and again in 41:28, "God has shown to Pharaoh what he is about to do." Joseph continued (41:32), "And the doubling of Pharaoh's dream means that the thing is fixed by God, and God will shortly bring it about." After correctly interpreting the dreams, Joseph was placed in charge of the distribution of grain. He had risen to the place of second only to the pharaoh in the Egyptian Empire. In the providence of God, the land of Palestine experienced a famine, and Jacob, hearing that there was grain in Egypt, sent his sons to purchase some. On the brothers' second trip to purchase additional grain, Joseph revealed himself to them. They returned to their land and told their father, Jacob, all that had transpired. As the family prepared to travel to Egypt, God appeared to Jacob.

> And God spoke to Israel in visions of the night and said, "Jacob, Jacob." And he said, "Here I am." Then he said, "I am God, the God of your father. Do not be afraid to go down to Egypt, for there I will make you into a great nation. I myself will go down with you to Egypt, and I will also bring you up again, and Joseph's hand shall close your eyes." (46:2–4)

God's revelation to Jacob came as a vision.

Jacob lived with his family in Egypt for many years. Near the end of his life, he bestowed blessings on his sons. Though it is not stated, the blessings that Jacob gave his sons (and grandsons) before his death in chapters 48–49 were prophetic words from God, though quite possibly not understood by the recipients as from God. At the end of Joseph's life, there was also a promise given to the rest of the family.

> And Joseph said to his brothers, "I am about to
> die, but God will visit you and bring you up out
> of this land to the land that he swore to Abraham,
> to Isaac, and to Jacob." Then Joseph made the
> sons of Israel swear, saying, "God will surely visit
> you, and you shall carry up my bones from here."
> (50:24–25)

The text of Genesis affirms the author's words in Hebrews 1:1–2 that "Long ago, at many times and in many ways, God spoke to our fathers by the prophets." At times the divine revelation from God came in visible form. At other times revelation from God came through a vision or a dream. As we have seen, to know with certainty the exact method of revelation may not be possible, but we know this is the Word of God.

4

God Speaks to Moses

We have examined God speaking the world into existence and having a "face-to-face" speaking relationship with Adam prior to the time of sin. After Adam sinned, there was a change in the manner in which God spoke. Man was banished from the garden and presumably no longer enjoyed the "face-to-face relationship" he had briefly experienced. That did not end revelation from God, but it did mean that something was different in the exchange of revelation from God to man.

Before us now is the remainder of the Law of Moses. We will survey God speaking in Exodus, Leviticus, Numbers, and Deuteronomy. Although we are not always told exactly how God communicated, we are given significant information which needs to be considered. It should be obvious that every word in the inspired text is a record of God speaking, but the emphasis in our study is to determine how He speaks.

We begin with God's message to Moses at the burning bush (Exod. 3:2 ff.). The first two chapters of Exodus provide a record of the partial fulfillment of the covenant God had made with Abraham in Genesis 15, as well as significant examples of the providence of God. The Israelite population had exploded, leading to a decree from the pharaoh to kill all of the male Israelite babies. Defiance by the midwives led to the sparing of baby Moses, resulting in Moses being raised in the house of Pharaoh. Providentially, Moses's own mother was hired by the daughter of the pharaoh to care for the boy. Through his mother's instruction, Moses was taught about the God of Israel. Moses was aware of his true identity; for as an adult, he defended a Hebrew against the abuse of an Egyptian, finally killing the Egyptian. He escaped into the land of Midian, where he was given a wife, and fathered children. During those forty years, the Hebrews were groaning and crying out to God to rescue them from slavery in Egypt. There is no record of God speaking during this forty-year period.

Moses continued to work for his father-in-law in the wilderness of Midian. It was there that the angel of the Lord appeared to Moses, "in a flame of fire out of the midst of a bush" (Exod. 3:2). That got his attention, so he took a closer look, and "God called to him out of the bush" (3:4). God appeared not as a man or an angel but as a flame of fire. This happened centuries earlier to Abraham when "a smoking fire pot and a flaming torch passed between these pieces" (Gen. 15:17).

In an audible voice, God called Moses's name and ordered him to remove his sandals, and then said, "I am the God of your father, the God of Abraham, the God of Isaac, and the God of Jacob" (Exod. 3:6). Moses hid his face, "for he was afraid to look at God" (3:6). He was no longer looking at a bush. God announced to Moses that He had seen the affliction of His people and heard their cry for help, and that He had come down to deliver them from the hand of the Egyptians and to take them to the land He had promised to Abraham's descendants. God told Moses, "Come, I will send you to Pharaoh that you may bring my people, the children of Israel, out of Egypt" (3:10). That message was received with overwhelming self-doubt.

Responding to Moses's complaint, God promised that He would be with Moses (v. 12), and He promised Moses a sign that he would return to serve the Lord on the very place where he was receiving this revelation. Moses continued to make excuses. In verse 14, God gave His own name to Moses, "I Am," and was told how to answer when the Israelites would ask who sent him: "Say this to the people of Israel, 'I am has sent me to you.'" This revelation continued:

> God also said to Moses, "Say this to the people
> of Israel: 'The LORD, the God of your fathers, the
> God of Abraham, the God of Isaac, and the God

of Jacob, has sent me to you.' This is my name forever, and thus I am to be remembered throughout all generations. Go and gather the elders of Israel together and say to them, 'The LORD, the God of your fathers, the God of Abraham, of Isaac, and of Jacob, has appeared to me, saying, "I have observed you and what has been done to you in Egypt, and I promise that I will bring you up out of the affliction of Egypt to the land of the Canaanites, the Hittites, the Amorites, the Perizzites, the Hivites, and the Jebusites, a land flowing with milk and honey."' And they will listen to your voice, and you and the elders of Israel shall go to the king of Egypt and say to him, 'The LORD, the God of the Hebrews, has met with us; and now, please let us go a three days' journey into the wilderness, that we may sacrifice to the LORD our God.' But I know that the king of Egypt will not let you go unless compelled by a mighty hand. So I will stretch out my hand and strike Egypt with all the wonders that I will do in it; after that he will let you go. And I will give this people favor in the sight of the Egyptians; and when you go, you shall not go empty, but each woman shall ask of her neighbor, and any woman who lives in her house, for silver and gold jewelry, and for clothing. You shall put them on your sons and on your daughters. So, you shall plunder the Egyptians." (vv. 15–22)

Moses's objections persisted, "They will not believe me or listen to my voice. They will say, 'The Lord did not appear to you'" (4:1). The Lord asked Moses what was in his hand and was told to throw his staff to the ground. When Moses did what God had ordered, the staff became a serpent, and Moses ran from it. God told Moses to grab the serpent's tail with his hand, and when he did, the serpent became a staff. The Lord then told Moses to place his hand inside his cloak and then take it out. His hand was leprous. When he repeated the process, his hand was restored. God continued,

> If they will not believe you…or listen to the first
> sign, they may believe the latter sign. If they will
> not believe even these two signs or listen to your
> voice, you shall take some water from the Nile
> and pour it on the dry ground, and the water that
> you shall take from the Nile will become blood
> on the dry ground. (4:8–9)

Still reluctant to believe and obey, Moses questioned God's choice by declaring himself "slow of speech and tongue" (4:10). God answered, "Who has made man's mouth? Who makes him mute, or deaf, or seeing, or blind? Is it not I, the LORD? Now therefore go, and I will be with your mouth and teach you what you shall speak" (vv. 11–12). Moses could only plead for the Lord to send someone else—anyone else. God, in anger, offered to send Aaron along with Moses; Aaron would act as Moses's mouthpiece.

Moses returned to his father-in-law to explain his intention to return to Egypt. God had revealed to Moses that those who had sought his life forty years earlier were now dead, so it was safe to return (4:19). The Lord continued to speak to Moses while in route, instructing Moses to do the miracles God had shown to him at the burning bush. The Lord warned Moses that He would harden Pharaoh's heart so that Pharaoh would refuse to let the Hebrew people go. The Lord also told Moses what to say to the Pharaoh:

> Thus says the LORD, "Israel is my firstborn son,
> and I say to you, 'Let my son go that he may
> serve me.' If you refuse to let him go, behold, I
> will kill your firstborn son." (vv. 22–23)

The Lord spoke also to Aaron telling him to meet Moses in the wilderness (4:27). Aaron did as he was instructed. When he met Moses, Moses told him all that the Lord had spoken to him. In Egypt, the elders of Israel were gathered together, and Aaron repeated the words that Moses had spoken to him. God's method of revelation to Moses and Aaron seems to have been by audible voice. Moses had heard God speak at the burning bush, and there is no indication that the method of revelation changed throughout the conversation between Moses and God.

Sadly, the complaints of Moses continued (5:22–23). He was responding to the frustration of the Israelites over the increased work demands from the pharaoh which resulted from Moses's request that the people be set free from their bondage. The Israelites were blaming Moses, and Moses was blaming God! Moses had to be reminded that deliverance would come.

> Now you shall see what I will do to Pharaoh; for with a strong hand he will send them out, and with a strong hand he will drive them out of his land...I am the LORD. (6:1–2)

The Lord reminded Moses that He had appeared to Abraham and Isaac and Jacob and had made a covenant with the patriarchs with regard to the land of Canaan. He had heard the groanings of His people, and it was time to remember that covenant. God instructed Moses to say to the people of Israel,

> I am the LORD, and I will bring you out from under the burdens of the Egyptians, and I will deliver you from slavery to them, and I will redeem you with an outstretched arm and with great acts of judgment. I will take you to be my people, and I will be your God, and you shall know that I am the LORD your God, who has brought you out from under the burdens of the Egyptians. I will bring you into the land that I swore to give to Abraham, to Isaac, and to Jacob. I will give it to you for a possession. I am the LORD. (Exod. 6:6–8)

Moses was then instructed to tell Pharaoh to let the people of Israel go. Moses argued that if the people of Israel had not believed him, why would the pharaoh listen to him? God did not answer the question but rather gave the order to carry our His instructions (6:13). The revelation came to both Aaron and Moses and seems to have been an audible, verbal communication.

To first harden and then eventually gain release from the pharaoh, God would bring upon the Egyptians ten plagues (Exod. 7:14 ff.). God said to Moses,

> See, I have made you like God to Pharaoh, and your brother Aaron shall be your prophet. You shall speak all that I command you, and your brother Aaron shall tell Pharaoh to let the people of Israel go out of his land. (7:1–2)

God's method of revelation to Pharaoh, to speak to Moses, who would then communicate to Aaron, who would then speak to the pharaoh, is likened as God's revelation from Himself to Moses to Aaron. The manner in which God would speak to and through His prophets was demonstrated here.

God made it clear that Pharaoh's heart would be hardened before he would finally allow the Israelites to set free. Even living through the experience of multiple signs and wonders, the pharaoh would refuse to listen. Nevertheless, as God laid His hand of judgment on Pharaoh and the Egyptians, they would finally come to know that God is the Lord (7:3–5). God instructed Moses and Aaron what to do when Pharaoh told them to prove themselves (7:9). He instructed Moses what to say with reference to each of the plagues.

In regard to the fourth plague, the plague of flies, God revealed to Moses that the land of Goshen, where the Israelites were dwelling, would be protected from the plagues that would come upon the Egyptians. The revelation of the seventh plague, the plague of hail, contained some specific warnings to Pharaoh but also some protections to the Egyptians if they believed what God was saying.

> For this time I will send all my plagues on you yourself, and on your servants and your people, so that you may know that there is none like me in all the earth. For by now I could have put out my hand and struck you and your people with pestilence, and you would have been cut off from the earth. But for this purpose I have raised you up, to show you my power, so that my name may be proclaimed in all the earth. You are still exalting yourself against my people and will not let them go. Behold, about this time tomorrow I will cause very heavy hail to fall, such as never has been in Egypt from the day it was founded until now. Now therefore send, get your livestock and all that you have in the field into safe shelter, for every man and beast that is in the field and is not brought home will die when the hail falls on them. (9:14–19)

The first part of the revelation of the eighth plague, the plague of locusts, contained a personal word to Moses and Aaron to provide a lasting testimony that truly God is the Lord. After Moses and Aaron left the presence of the pharaoh, the servants of the king pleaded with him to let the Israelites go and serve their Lord, acknowledging that what God was doing was bringing Egypt to ruin (10:7). Pharaoh called Moses and Aaron back but refused their terms; they were thrown out of his presence.

After the plague of darkness, the Lord revealed to Moses that there would be one final plague which would result in Pharaoh allowing the Israelites to leave Egypt. Moses was to speak to the people so they would be prepared to leave quickly. The people were instructed to ask the Egyptians for silver and gold, assured that the people of

Egypt would give it to them (11:2–3; 12:35–36). This promise from the Lord had been first given to Abraham:

> They will be afflicted for four hundred years. But I will bring judgment on the nation that they serve, and afterward they shall come out with great possessions. (Gen. 15:14)

Part of that prophesied judgment, the killing of the firstborn, had been communicated to Pharaoh when Moses first approached him requesting the release of the people of Israel:

> Then you shall say to Pharaoh, "Thus says the LORD, Israel is my firstborn son, and I say to you, 'Let my son go that he may serve me.' If you refuse to let him go, behold, I will kill your firstborn son." (Exod. 4:22–23)

That promise was soon to be fulfilled. The tenth plague was recorded in Exodus 12:29–32. We are not told how God spoke to Moses regarding the plagues and Israel's deliverance, but it seems reasonable to assume that the communication was audible.

God's message concerning the Passover was recorded in Exodus 12:1 ff. The first twenty verses of the chapter were God's revelation to Moses and Aaron regarding the institution of the Passover. This may have been a voice from the Lord to the two men, or it could have been revealed to Moses and relayed to Aaron. This first Passover would be the final meal in Egypt for the Israelites before their exodus. The tenth plague would occur only hours after the feast, and the Israelites would finally be set free from Pharaoh's tyranny. These instructions would guide the Israelites for generations (12:17).

The month of the exodus would be marked as the first month of the year (12:2). It was on the fourteenth day of this month that things would happen quickly. The Lord spoke to Moses to consecrate all the firstborn, both man and beast (13:1–2). The Feast of Unleavened Bread was instituted (13:3–16). Moses gave to the

Israelites a prophetic word from the Lord. This may have been the relay of a direct communication from the Lord, or it may have been the words of Moses that were guided by the Spirit to communicate the Word of the Lord much like the process indicated in 2 Peter 1:20–21. As the people escaped Egypt, they followed the Lord's leading, as He provided a cloud by day and a fire by night to lead them (13:21). Moses interjected the reason for the direction God led them:

> For God said, "Lest the people change their minds when they see war and return to Egypt."
> But God led the people around by the way of the wilderness toward the Red Sea. (13:17–18)

As the people made haste from the land of Egypt, God began to make clear His revelation regarding the crossing of the Red Sea and the beginning of the wilderness journey (Exod. 14:1 ff.). Chapter 14 opened with revelation from the Lord to Moses regarding the maneuver they were to make that would cause Pharaoh to believe that Israel was wandering without direction. God told Moses He would harden the heart of Pharaoh causing him to pursue the Israelites. This was designed by God to gain glory for Himself and to show the Egyptians that He was the Lord (14:1–4). When the Israelites realized that the Egyptian army was pursuing them, they panicked and complained to Moses. Even while Moses was giving a speech to the people not to be afraid and to stand firm and know that the Lord would fight for them, he apparently was saying something else to the Lord! In 14:15, "The Lord said to Moses, 'Why do you cry to me? Tell the people of Israel to go forward.'" The Lord gave Moses instructions regarding his staff and the dividing of the Red Sea. Verse 19 spoke of the presence of the angel of the Lord. He could have been the one speaking in 14:15–18. In verse 26, the Lord spoke again, "Stretch out your hand over the sea, that the water may come back upon the Egyptians, upon their chariots, and upon their horsemen."

Shortly after the great victory over Egypt at the Red Sea, the people began to complain because there was no water. When they came to Mara, the water was bitter, increasing their grumbling.

Words from the Lord were recorded by Moses, but there is no indication how they were given.

> If you will diligently listen to the voice of the LORD your God, and do that which is right in his eyes, and give ear to his commandments and keep all his statutes, I will put none of the diseases on you that I put on the Egyptians, for I am the LORD, your healer. (Exod. 15:26)

God communicated His message concerning manna from heaven and water from the rock in Exodus 16–17. The people were grumbling about a lack of food. The Lord spoke to Moses,

> Behold, I am about to rain bread from heaven for you, and the people shall go out and gather a day's portion every day, that I may test them, whether they will walk in my law or not. On the sixth day, when they prepare what they bring in, it will be twice as much as they gather daily. (16:4–5).

And again, the Lord spoke to Moses,

> I have heard the grumbling of the people of Israel. Say to them, "At twilight you shall eat meat, and in the morning, you shall be filled with bread. Then you shall know that I am the LORD your God." (16:12)

At the end of chapter 16, Moses spoke of further revelation he had received regarding the preservation of a jar of manna that would be a testimony to the Lord's gracious provision (16:32–34). In chapter 17, the people were once again without water and were quarreling with Moses to do something about it. Moses brought the complaint to the Lord, presumably in prayer. The Lord answered Moses with instructions to take some of the elders with him and to go to Horeb and, with his staff, strike the rock there, and it would produce water (17:6). The Lord promised to be with Moses at Horeb. Later the Amalekites fought against Israel. Under the leadership of Joshua, Israel defeated Amalek and his army. After the victory, the Lord spoke to Moses,

> Write this as a memorial in a book and recite it in the ears of Joshua, that I will utterly blot out the memory of Amalek from under heaven. (17:14)

God led the children of Israel into the wilderness of Sinai on their way to the promised land. Leaving the people at the foot of the mountain, Moses ascended the heights where God extensively spoke to him (19:3–6, 9 ff.; note v. 19. Compare with Deut. 5:4 ff.). The Lord said to Moses, "Behold, I am coming to you in a thick cloud, that the people may hear when I speak with you and may also believe you forever" (Exod. 19:9). A series of revelations from the Lord to Moses continued to the end of the chapter. What Moses personally received, he later relayed to the people. It is significant to note that these revelations from God, in whatever form, were given directly to Moses. God's message to the people came through Moses as he relayed God's words to them. This pattern is consistent throughout the books of Moses.

> Now when all the people saw the thunder and the flashes of lightning and the sound of the trumpet and the mountain smoking, the people were afraid and trembled, and they stood far off and said to Moses, "You speak to us, and we will listen; but do not let God speak to us, lest we die." Moses said to the people, "Do not fear, for God has come to test you, that the fear of him may be before you, that you may not sin." The people stood far off, while Moses drew near to the thick darkness where God was. (20:18–21)

Chapters 20 through 31 record the giving of the Law to the children of Israel. The Ten Commandments were recorded in 20:1–17. Then God instructed Moses to say to the people, "You have seen for yourselves that I have talked with you from heaven" (20:22). Once again, we see that when Moses relayed the message he had received from God, the Israelites regarded the message as from God, not from Moses.

In the midst of God revealing the law to Moses, God spoke instructions regarding entrance into the promised land:

> Behold, I send an angel before you to guard you on the way and to bring you to the place that I have prepared. Pay careful attention to him and obey his voice; do not rebel against him, for he will not pardon your transgression, for my name is in him. (23:20–21)

Chapter 24 begins with the revelation of Moses's position in relation to the other leaders in Israel.

> Come up to the LORD, you and Aaron, Nadab, and Abihu, and seventy of the elders of Israel, and worship from afar. Moses alone shall come near to the LORD, but the others shall not come near, and the people shall not come up with him. (vv. 1–2)

Verses 3 and 4 express how God's revelation was preserved.

> Moses came and told the people all the words of the LORD and all the rules. And all the people answered with one voice and said, "All the words that the LORD has spoken we will do." And Moses wrote down all the words of the LORD.

In verse 9, the individuals mentioned, "went up and they saw the God of Israel...they beheld God, and they ate and drank" (24:10–11). Moses was then called to come further and receive the tablets of stone (24:12). The revelation continued through chapter 30 with detailed instructions concerning the tabernacle and the various pieces of furniture to be placed within the tabernacle, as well as the description of the priestly garments and the articulation of priestly duties. Urim and Thummim were also introduced.

> So Aaron shall bear the names of the sons of Israel in the breastpiece of judgment on his heart, when he goes into the Holy Place, to bring them to regular remembrance before the LORD. And in the breastpiece of judgment you shall put the Urim and the Thummim, and they shall be on Aaron's heart, when he goes in before the LORD. Thus Aaron shall bear the judgment of the people of Israel on his heart before the LORD regularly. (28:29–30)

The Lord identified two men He had filled with His Spirit, giving them exceptional ability to make the things God had revealed and described (31:1–6). While it is impossible to be certain, this communication appears to have been in some sense "face-to-face." The final verse of chapter 31 strongly supports this position:

> And he gave to Moses, when he had finished speaking with him on Mount Sinai, the two tablets of the testimony, tablets of stone, written with the finger of God.

It would be difficult to image how Moses could have received the tablets of stone without some sort of exchange from God.

While Moses was on the mountain with the Lord, the Israelites, under the leadership of Aaron, had descended into idol worship. God revealed to Moses what was happening at the bottom of the mountain and declared His intention to "consume them" (32:10). Moses pleaded for the lives of the people based on maintaining the reputation of God's name. He then descended the mountain with the two tablets of stone. Seeing the golden calf and the people's behavior, "he threw the tablets out of his hands and broke them at the foot of the mountain" (32:19). Moses asked, "Who is on the Lord's side? Come to me." He then said,

> Thus says the Lord God of Israel, "Put your sword on your side each of you and go to and fro from gate to gate throughout the camp, and each of you kill his brother and his companion and his neighbor." (32:27)

The next day Moses asked the Lord to forgive the sins of the people:

> "But if not, please blot me out of your book that you have written." But the LORD said to Moses, "Whoever has sinned against me, I will blot out of my book. But now go, lead the people to the place about which I have spoken to you; behold, my angel shall go before you. Nevertheless, in the day when I visit, I will visit their sin upon them." (32:32–34)

God continued to speak to Moses revealing aspects of His presence and His glory (Exod. 33). God also gave Moses instructions concerning the replacement of the broken tablets (34:1 ff.). The Lord told Moses to depart and move toward the land of Canaan. He promised to send His angel before them and to drive out the Canaanites from the land (33:2). Verse 11 is instructive. "Thus the LORD used to speak to Moses face to face, as a man speaks to his friend." This suggests that most of the time when God spoke to Moses, it was in some sense "face-to-face." However, that "face-to-face" encounter was qualified by the conversation and demonstration between Moses and God in verses 12–23. Moses was asking for clarity, and God responded, "My presence will go with you and I will give you rest" (v. 14). Note what follows:

> Moses said, "Please show me your glory." And he said, "I will make all my goodness pass before you and will proclaim before you my name 'The LORD.' And I will be gracious to whom I will be gracious, and will show mercy on whom I will show mercy. But," he said, "you cannot see my face, for man shall not see me and live." (vv. 18–20)

The Lord allowed Moses to hide himself in a cleft in a rock, and He promised to cover Moses with His hand until He had passed by. He would them remove His hand. God told Moses, "You shall see my back, but my face shall not be seen" (33:23). Following some instructions recorded in chapter 34, we are told that the Lord "descended in the cloud and stood with him there" (v. 5). The covenant was renewed as the Lord spoke (34:10 ff.). Then the Lord instructed Moses to "Write these words, for in accordance with these words I have made a covenant with you and with Israel" (v. 27).

God provided Moses with direction for the erecting of the tabernacle and the consecration of it (40:1 ff.). The book of Exodus ends with God coming in a cloud and filling the tabernacle. Apparently that same cloud would arise and move as God directed the children of Israel throughout the wilderness. This continued until they were ready to enter the land of promise some four decades later.

> Then the cloud covered the tent of meeting, and the glory of the LORD filled the tabernacle. And Moses was not able to enter the tent of meeting because the cloud settled on it, and the glory of the LORD filled the tabernacle. Throughout all their journeys, whenever the cloud was taken up from over the tabernacle, the people of Israel

would set out. But if the cloud was not taken up, then they did not set out till the day that it was taken up. For the cloud of the LORD was on the tabernacle by day, and fire was in it by night, in the sight of all the house of Israel throughout all their journeys. (40:34–38)

The cloud was more of a guide than specific revelation.

God often spoke to Moses from the tent of meeting concerning offerings, sacrifices, ordination, clean and unclean issues, feast days, intentional and unintentional sin, etc. (see Lev. 1:1 ff.; 4:1; 5:14; 6:1, 8, 19, 24; 7:22, 28; 8:1; 10:8; 12:1; 13:1; 14:1, 33; 15:1; 16:1; 17:1; 18:1; 19:1; 20:1; 21:1, 16; 22:1, 26; 23:1, 9, 23, 26, 33; 24:1, 13; 25:1; 27:1). The book of Leviticus ends with, "These are the commandments that the LORD commanded Moses for the people of Israel on Mount Sinai" (27:34). Nearly the entire book of Leviticus is the Lord speaking directly to Moses with instruction to either give the revelation to Aaron so that he could to tell the people of Israel or to personally communicate the message from God to the people. Moses was the prophet to whom God spoke, and he would then speak to the people the words that God had given him. These words that he spoke were recorded by him and preserved by God in order that future generations would have this divine revelation. Once again, it is important to remember that there is little, if any, revelation, that came directly from God to the people. The revelation Moses received from God at Sinai involved some sort of a meeting between Moses and God on the mountain.

There are some references of the Lord speaking to Aaron (as in Lev. 10:8, 18:1), but generally the Lord's words were to Moses or Moses and Aaron together (11:1, 13:1, 14:33; Num. 2:1, 4:1). The revelation of God in the OT consistently came as the author of the book of Hebrews described: "Long ago, at many times and in many ways, God spoke to our fathers by the prophets." Moses was the prophet through whom God revealed Himself and His will for His people.

God gave Moses revelation concerning taking a census, arranging the camp (Num. 1:1, 48; 2:1), directing the Levites (3:5, 11, 14, 40, 44; 4:1, 21), and instructions dealing with people's uncleanness and sin (5:1, 5, 11). God also instructed Moses in regard to Nazarite vows (6:1) and the revelation of God's blessings upon His people.

> The LORD bless you and keep you; the LORD make his face to shine upon you and be gracious to you; the LORD lift up his countenance upon you and give you peace. (6:24–26)

According to Numbers 7:89,

> And when Moses went into the tent of meeting to speak with the LORD, he heard the voice speaking to him from above the mercy seat that was on the ark of the testimony, from between the two cherubim; and it spoke to him.

This was an audible voice from God to Moses (note also Numbers 8:1, 5, 23; 9:1, 9). In relation to directing the Israelites in their travels, God "spoke" to them with a cloud/fire.

> Sometimes the cloud was a few days over the tabernacle, and according to the command of the LORD they remained in camp; then according to the command of the LORD they set out. And sometimes the cloud remained from evening until morning. And when the cloud lifted in the morning, they set out, or if it continued for a day and a night, when the cloud lifted they set out. Whether it was two days, or a month, or a longer time, that the cloud continued over the tabernacle, abiding there, the people of Israel remained in camp and did not set out, but when it lifted they set out. At the command of the LORD they

camped, and at the command of the LORD they set out. They kept the charge of the LORD, at the command of the LORD by Moses. (vv. 20–23)

The Lord, through Moses, provided a demonstration of how this was accomplished.

So they set out from the mount of the LORD three days' journey. And the ark of the covenant of the LORD went before them three days' journey, to seek out a resting place for them. And the cloud of the LORD was over them by day, whenever they set out from the camp. And whenever the ark set out, Moses said, "Arise, O LORD, and let your enemies be scattered, and let those who hate you flee before you." And when it rested, he said, "Return, O LORD, to the ten thousand thousands of Israel." (10:33–36)

Though God miraculously cared for the children of Israel, the wilderness wanderings were filled with complaints and disobedience, which resulted in the direct judgment by the Lord (11:1). The judgment prompted the people to cry out to Moses, that he might plead with God to stop! Moses prayed, and the fiery judgment died down, but the people's complaints returned in relation to their constant diet of manna; they actually wept over the divine menu! They demanded meat! Moses was angry and frustrated by the people's reaction and became angry and frustrated with God, angry enough to demand that God take his life (11:11–15)! God answered, providing the people's demands, even though Moses doubted (11:16 ff.).

Miriam and Aaron were unhappy with Moses's choice of a wife, so they challenged Moses's leadership. As the Lord interrupted and corrected their argument, further insight can be found concerning the methods of God's revelation. Aaron and Miriam argued,

> "Has the LORD indeed spoken only through Moses? Has he not spoken through us also?" And the LORD heard it. Now the man Moses was very meek, more than all people who were on the face of the earth. And suddenly the LORD said to Moses and to Aaron and Miriam, "Come out, you three, to the tent of meeting." And the three of them came out. And the LORD came down in a pillar of cloud and stood at the entrance of the tent and called Aaron and Miriam, and they both came forward. And he said, "Hear my words: If there is a prophet among you, I the LORD make myself known to him in a vision; I speak with him in a dream. Not so with my servant Moses. He is faithful in all my house. With him I speak mouth to mouth, clearly, and not in riddles, and he beholds the form of the LORD. Why then were you not afraid to speak against my servant Moses?" (Num. 12:2–8)

God was speaking, and the three heard what He was saying. God expressed the general method He used to speak to prophets, in dreams and visions, but His revelation to Moses had been "mouth to mouth." After speaking to the three, God brought a leprous judgment against Miriam (12:13–14).

After traveling a relatively short time, the Israelites arrived at the outskirts of the territory God had promised. He provided instructions through Moses for scouting the land (Num. 13 ff.). Moses was instructed to send spies into the area so that they might see what God had promised. The land was certainly as God had described, but the message from the majority was not to proceed. The enemy was insurmountable. The people began to grumble and rebel and were ready to choose another leader to return to Egypt (14:4). Moses and Aaron pleaded with the people to reconsider. They were preparing to stone Moses and Aaron when the Lord intervened. Speaking to Moses, the Lord promised judgment for the Israelites' unbelief (14:11–12). Moses pleaded for mercy in order to preserve the Lord's name and reputation. Though the people would be spared immediate judgment, none of the adults would enter the promised land except Caleb and Joshua (14:20–35), the two who gave the minority report about entering the land. Further instructions were given to Moses regarding when they would come into the land. These would be recorded but would not be reality for four decades (15:1, 17, 37).

Unrest, rebellion, and confusion continued (Num. 16). A coup, led by Korah, was attempted against Moses and Aaron. The Lord spoke to His two leaders calling for a separation between the people and Korah and his followers (16:20). The ground opened and literally swallowed the rebellion (16:31–35). In chapter 17, still dealing with leadership issues, God spoke to Moses instructing him to gather staffs from the leaders of the people. Aaron's staff budded and bore ripe almonds. The Lord instructed Moses to keep Aaron's staff "as a sign for the rebels, that you may make an end of their grumblings against me, lest they die" (17:10). That staff was kept in the ark of the covenant as a sign and warning against future grumblings! The Lord spoke to Aaron in chapter 18 regarding the duties of the priests and Levites (18:1, 8). Additional information was given to Moses (18:25) and to both men (19:1) concerning laws for purification.

Chapter 20 opens with a water shortage and another rebellion against Moses and Aaron. The two leaders fell on their faces before the Lord at the tent of meeting. There, the "glory of the Lord appeared to them and the Lord spoke to Moses" (20:7). The instructions were clear, "take the staff...assemble the congregation...tell the rock...to yield its water." That was not what happened. The Lord reprimanded Moses and Aaron:

> Because you did not believe in me, to uphold me
> as holy in the eyes of the people of Israel, there-
> fore you shall not bring this assembly into the
> land that I have given them. (20:12)

Before the end of the chapter, the Lord spoke to Moses and Aaron again. Aaron was stripped of his priestly garments, and they were transferred to Eleazar, Aaron's son, and Aaron died on the mountain (20:28). Even with all that had transpired, the people again spoke against the Lord and against Moses, still complaining about the manna: "we loath this worthless food" (21:5). The Lord sent "fiery serpents" among the people and many died. Moses prayed and God answered. "Make a fiery serpent and set it on a pole, and everyone who is bitten, when he sees it, shall live" (v. 8). This strange account will surface again in the Gospel of John referring directly to the Lord Jesus on the cross (John 3).

In Numbers 22–24, we are introduced to the prophet Balaam. God did speak through Balaam even though he was a prophet for hire, willing to prophesy judgment upon his own people for a price, and the pagan king of Moab was willing to pay. In chapter 22:9, the text tells us that God came to Balaam, and in verse 22, "the angel of the Lord" stood in his way. Balaam was not able to see the angel of the Lord, but the donkey on which he was riding could! The text used the phrase, "the angel of the Lord" in verses 22, 24, 25, 26, 27, 31, 32, 34, and 35, but in verses 28 and 31, it is the Lord who opened the mouth of the donkey and who opened the eyes of Balaam so he was able to see the angel of the Lord. We will consider the identity of the angel of the Lord a little later, but it should be apparent that the Lord and the angel of the Lord were one and the same.

In chapter 23, "God met Balaam…and the Lord put a word in Balaam's mouth" (23:4–5). In verse 2 of the next chapter, Balaam was speaking the word of the Lord as the Spirit gave him utterance, "The Spirit of God came upon him and he took up his discourse and said." Balaam's final oracle included,

> I see him, but not now; I behold him, but not near: a star shall come out of Jacob, and a scepter shall rise out of Israel; it shall crush the forehead of Moab and break down all the sons of Sheth. (24:17)

This prophecy most likely referred to the Lord Jesus Christ. From this we gain some insight into the manner in which God gave revelation to His prophets, coming upon them and putting words in their mouths. We will see this later in the major and minor prophets.

God continued His revelation to Moses (25:10, 16, 26:1). It should be noted here that the Lord was now speaking to Moses and Eleazar, Aaron's son, now that Aaron had died (26:52; 27:6, 12, 18; 28:1 ff.; 30:16; 31:1, 25; 34:1, 16; 35:1, 9).

Much of Deuteronomy is a review of what God had already revealed to Moses. Such phrases as, "The Lord our God said to us," indicate previous revelation (Deut. 1:6, 21, 42; 3:26; 4:12; 5:6). Deuteronomy 4:12 is instructive with reference to what the people heard and saw at the time of the giving of the Ten Commandments, "Then the LORD spoke to you out of the midst of the fire. You heard the sound of words but saw no form; there was only a voice." In the following chapter, Moses told the people,

> The LORD spoke with you face to face at the
> mountain, out of the midst of the fire, while I
> stood between the LORD and you at that time,
> to declare to you the word of the LORD. For you
> were afraid because of the fire, and you did not
> go up into the mountain. (5:4–5)

Moses continued making known what God had revealed as he quoted the Ten Commandments. He explained and clarified what took place at the mountain when the Ten Commandments were given.

> These words the LORD spoke to all your assembly
> at the mountain out of the midst of the fire, the
> cloud, and the thick darkness, with a loud voice;
> and he added no more. And he wrote them on
> two tablets of stone and gave them to me. And
> as soon as you heard the voice out of the midst
> of the darkness, while the mountain was burn-

> ing with fire, you came near to me, all the heads
> of your tribes, and your elders. And you said,
> "Behold, the LORD our God has shown us his
> glory and greatness, and we have heard his voice
> out of the midst of the fire. This day we have
> seen God speak with man, and man still live."
> (5:22–24)

This was one of those rare occasions when the people at large heard the voice of God speak.

Included in Moses's prophetic utterances to the new generation entering the promised land were declarations such as, "Hear, O Israel, The Lord our God, the Lord is one" (6:4). There is interesting insight in the exchange between God and Moses, as Moses shared his remembrance at the mountain when the people made the golden calf (9:13 ff.). Moses also presented important insight with relation to the ministry of prophets and their prophecies in chapter 18.

> The LORD your God will raise up for you a
> prophet like me from among you, from your
> brothers—it is to him you shall listen—just as
> you desired of the LORD your God at Horeb on
> the day of the assembly, when you said, "Let me
> not hear again the voice of the LORD my God or
> see this great fire any more, lest I die." And the
> LORD said to me, "They are right in what they
> have spoken. I will raise up for them a prophet
> like you from among their brothers. And I will
> put my words in his mouth, and he shall speak
> to them all that I command him. And whoever
> will not listen to my words that he shall speak
> in my name, I myself will require it of him. But
> the prophet who presumes to speak a word in my
> name that I have not commanded him to speak,
> or who speaks in the name of other gods, that
> same prophet shall die." And if you say in your

heart, "How may we know the word that the LORD has not spoken?"—when a prophet speaks in the name of the LORD, if the word does not come to pass or come true, that is a word that the LORD has not spoken; the prophet has spoken it presumptuously. You need not be afraid of him. (18:15–22)

Based on God's revelation that Moses had received, mostly at Sinai, Moses instructed the new generation of Israelites who were about to enter the promised land. Moses believed that what he had been teaching was from the Lord.

This day the LORD your God commands you to do these statutes and rules. You shall therefore be careful to do them with all your heart and with all your soul. You have declared today that the LORD is your God, and that you will walk in his ways, and keep his statutes and his commandments and his rules and will obey his voice. And the LORD has declared today that you are a people for his treasured possession, as he has promised you, and that you are to keep all his commandments, and that he will set you in praise and in fame and in honor high above all nations that he has made, and that you shall be a people holy to the LORD your God, as he promised. (Deut. 26:16–19).

Moses affirmed in 29:1 that this renewal of the covenant came at the command of God. He affirmed God's revelation in 29:29:

The secret things belong to the LORD our God, but the things that are revealed belong to us and to our children forever, that we may do all the words of this law. (Deut. 29:29)

The recording of God's Law was credited to Moses.

> Then Moses wrote this law and gave it to the priests,
> the sons of Levi, who carried the ark of the covenant
> of the LORD, and to all the elders of Israel. (31:9)

God's message to Moses about his death and to Joshua with regard to taking the place of Moses to lead the Israelites was recorded in Deuteronomy 31:16–23. Moses was instructed to write "this song" and teach it to the people. Presumably God revealed the words, and Moses recorded it. Moses also recorded the instructions that God had given to him regarding his death.

> That very day the LORD spoke to Moses, "Go
> up this mountain of the Abarim, Mount Nebo,
> which is in the land of Moab, opposite Jericho,
> and view the land of Canaan, which I am giving
> to the people of Israel for a possession. And die
> on the mountain which you go up, and be gath-
> ered to your people, as Aaron your brother died
> in Mount Hor and was gathered to his people,
> because you broke faith with me in the midst
> of the people of Israel at the waters of Meribah-
> kadesh, in the wilderness of Zin, and because
> you did not treat me as holy in the midst of the
> people of Israel. For you shall see the land before
> you, but you shall not go there, into the land that
> I am giving to the people of Israel." (32:48–52)

It is likely that Joshua recorded the actual event of Moses's death (Deut. 34:1–8), presumably receiving this revelation from God, since no one was present when Moses died and was buried. God's words regarding His servant, Moses, were,

> And the LORD said to him, "This is the land of
> which I swore to Abraham, to Isaac, and to Jacob,

'I will give it to your offspring.' I have let you
see it with your eyes, but you shall not go over
there." (34:4)

And the text says that God "buried him in the valley in the land
of Moab…no one knows the place of his burial" (34:5–6).

The author of Hebrews made it clear that in the OT, God would
speak through prophets. The first five books of the OT were recorded
by Moses who was declared by God to be His prophet. In the final
chapter of Deuteronomy, God said,

And there has not arisen a prophet since in Israel
like Moses, whom the LORD knew face to face,
none like him for all the signs and the wonders
that the LORD sent him to do in the land of
Egypt, to Pharaoh and to all his servants and to
all his land, and for all the mighty power and all
the great deeds of terror that Moses did in the
sight of all Israel. (34:10–12)

5

God Speaks throughout the
Historical Record of Israel

God's revelation continued as He spoke to Joshua and to the judges who were raised up by Him to lead His people. The final judge, Samuel, also heard from God as the monarchy of Israel was being established. First Saul, then David, and finally Solomon ruled the united monarchy of Israel. The kingdom was divided when Solomon's son, Rehoboam, assumed the throne. The divided monarchy, as the northern and southern kingdoms of Israel, met disaster and defeat. The northern kingdom abandoned the God of Israel and was destroyed by the Assyrian Empire in 722 BC. The southern kingdom fell to the Babylonian Empire one hundred thirty or so years later (586 BC). God restored the southern kingdom, as a remnant of Israelites returned to the land, but the nation (Judah) continued to be under the thumb of a foreign power for the remainder of biblical history. Yet through it all, God, from time to time, continued to speak.

We begin this historical section with an examination of God speaking to Joshua, as God gave His servant instructions regarding the entrance into the land, and the conquest of that land, which God had promised to His people. God's Word was spoken primarily to Moses from the time of the burning bush until the time of his death. Now God spoke to Joshua, the new leader of the Israelites. The book of Joshua begins with God speaking, reiterating the promises He had given to Moses regarding the land. Joshua affirmed both the value of God's revelation given to Moses and its divine authorship.

> This Book of the Law shall not depart from your mouth, but you shall meditate on it day and night, so that you may be careful to do according to all that is written in it. For then you will make your way prosperous, and then you will have good success. (Josh. 1:8)

Joshua was quoting Moses as the word of the Lord (1:13 ff.).

The Lord confirmed Joshua as the legitimate and chosen leader of the nation and promised to be with him as He was with Moses. The Lord revealed to Joshua what he needed to know concerning the crossing of the Jordan River and the role the priests were to assume with regard to the ark of the covenant. How God communicated to Joshua, we are not told, but Joshua was certain this was from the Lord. He called the people together, "Come here and listen to the words of the Lord your God" (3:9). What Joshua said to the people was revelation from the Lord, and what they heard was God speaking even though it was coming from Joshua's mouth.

After the people crossed the Jordan, the Lord spoke to Joshua regarding the building of a monument from stones secured from the dry riverbed, before the waters returned to their normal course. The river was being held back by the Lord (4:1 ff. with vv. 15–16). The Lord also gave revelation in regard to the covenant of circumcision. Before the conquest of the land began, obedience to the law of circumcision had ceased. The generation born in the wilderness had not kept this law (5:5). After Joshua called the people to obedience and the surgeries were completed, God said to Joshua, "Today I have rolled away the reproach of Egypt from you" (v. 9). While the Israelites remained in the camp at Gilgal, they observed Passover. On the following day, the forty-year daily supply of manna ceased. Available to them now was the fruit of the land of Canaan (vv. 11–12).

Just before the Israelites began the conquest of the land, Joshua had an encounter with the "commander of the army of the Lord"

(5:13–15); Joshua "lifted up his eyes and looked, and behold, a man was standing before him" (v. 15). Though the identity of the man was not given, Joshua "fell on his face to the earth and worshiped," and the man did not stop him. It is instructive to compare Joshua's experience with that of Moses at the burning bush. God commanded Moses,

> Do not come near; take your sandals off your feet, for the place on which you are standing is holy ground. (Exod. 3:5)

With regard to Joshua,

> And the commander of the Lord's army said to Joshua, "Take off your sandals from your feet, for the place where you are standing is holy." And Joshua did so. (Josh. 5:15)

It seems reasonable to conclude that the commander of the army of the Lord who had appeared to Joshua was the pre-incarnate Christ.

Following the encounter with the commander of the army of the Lord, the Lord spoke to Joshua, not only assuring him of victory which the Lord would give the Israelites over Jericho but also explaining the manner in which the victory would be won (Josh. 6:2–5). As the Israelites prepared to make their final day's march around the city, Joshua spoke a warning to the people that Jericho, and all of its possessions were to be "devoted to the Lord for destruction" (6:17–21). Joshua's warnings regarding the spoils of Jericho as being devoted to the Lord, no doubt came as a result of revelation from God to Joshua, although the exchange between the Lord and Joshua is not recorded.

God brought down the walls of the city of Jericho giving Israel a great victory in their initial conquest. Next in line was the small city of Ai. Joshua thought it unnecessary to send the entire army, settling on a militia of three thousand soldiers. The Israelite army was driven back, and thirty-six men were lost in the battle. Joshua cried out to the Lord in a complaint against God for not protecting Israel and failing to grant victory. God spoke.

> Get up! Why have you fallen on your face? Israel has sinned; they have transgressed my covenant that I commanded them; they have taken some of the devoted things; they have stolen and lied and put them among their own belongings. Therefore the people of Israel cannot stand before their enemies. They turn their backs before their enemies because they have become devoted for destruction. I will be with you no more unless you destroy the devoted things from among you. (7:10–12)

It is interesting to note that though God had identified the transgression, He did not identify the transgressors. Instead He gave instructions to bring the people tribe by tribe, and then once the tribe was identified, clan by clan, and once the clan was identified, household by household, until the transgressor was identified. All of this was to be revealed by lot, not by direct revelation from God.

Having dealt with the reason for the defeat, the Israelites prepared to attack Ai a second time. Following the Lord's instructions, Ai was soundly defeated. "Joshua burned Ai and made it forever a heap of ruins" (8:28). Following the victory, Joshua read the words of the Lord from the Book of the Law. This was God speaking, but here, it was through the revelation that came through the Law which Moses had recorded.

> And afterward he read all the words of the law, the blessing and the curse, according to all that is written in the Book of the Law. There was not a word of all that Moses commanded that Joshua did not read before all the assembly of Israel, and

the women, and the little ones, and the sojourn-
ers who lived among them. (8:34–35)

A large army made up of militias from several city-states
encamped together, ready to fight against Israel (Josh. 11). The Lord
instructed Joshua not to be afraid. The Lord not only promised victory but also instructed Joshua to hamstring the horses and burn the
chariots with fire. This was a graphic reminder for Israel not to place
their confidence in the weapons of war but in the name of the Lord!
Years later, King David would write this warning:

Some trust in chariots and some in horses, but
we trust in the name of the LORD our God. They
collapse and fall, but we rise and stand upright.
(Ps. 20:7–8)

Throughout Joshua's life, the Lord continued to speak to His
servant,

Now Joshua was old and advanced in years, and
the LORD said to him, "You are old and advanced
in years, and there remains yet very much land to
possess." (13:1)

The method of the revelation, however, was not indicated.

As the conquest and settlement of the land continued, God
gave Joshua information concerning the establishment of the cities
of refuge: "The Lord said to Joshua, 'Say to the people of Israel.'"
Interesting here is what the Lord said with reference to the words
recorded by Moses, "Appoint the cities of refuge, of which I spoke
to you through Moses." This was affirmation of the Lord speaking
through what was recorded. Joshua wrote, "Not one word of all the
good promises that the Lord had made to the house of Israel had
failed; all came to pass" (21:45). Before his death, Joshua spoke a
lengthy quotation from the Lord (24:2–13) and then recorded those
words in the Book of the Law of God (24:26).

After Joshua's death, there was a leadership vacuum. It is unclear who specifically inquired of the Lord or how they did so, but the question was asked, "Who shall go up first for us against the Canaanites to fight against them?" (Judg. 1:1). The Lord's answer came through the angel of the Lord.

> Now the angel of the LORD...said, "I brought you up from Egypt and brought you into the land that I swore to give to your fathers. I said, 'I will never break my covenant with you, and you shall make no covenant with the inhabitants of this land; you shall break down their altars.' But you have not obeyed my voice. What is this you have done? So now I say, I will not drive them out before you, but they shall become thorns in your sides, and their gods shall be a snare to you." As soon as the angel of the LORD spoke these words to all the people of Israel, the people lifted up their voices and wept. (Judg. 2:1–5).

This was not the first time the angel of the Lord had appeared. The words spoken were received with sorrow and sacrifice. What the angel of the Lord said would be unveiled in the sad events recorded by the judges.

Judge Deborah, a prophetess, was introduced in Judges 4. She told Barak,

> Has not the LORD, the God of Israel, commanded you, "Go, gather your men at Mount Tabor, taking 10,000 from the people of Naphtali and the people of Zebulun. And I will draw out Sisera, the general of Jabin's army, to meet you by the river Kishon with his chariots and his troops, and I will give him into your hand"? (4:6–7)

Deborah prophesied that because of Barak's reluctance, he would receive no glory, but that the enemy, Sisera, would be defeated at the hand of a woman. How Deborah received this prophetic word, we are not told.

The next occurrence of the Lord speaking was through an unnamed prophet (Judg. 6:7–8) and again through the angel of the Lord (6:11). As has been observed, "the angel of the Lord" (v. 11) and "the Lord" (vv. 14, 16) appear to be the same individual. That the angel of the Lord "came" and "sat under the terebinth" strongly suggests that this message from God came directly to Gideon. This entire passage indicates a "face-to-face" encounter between Gideon and the Lord (6:18–21; 6:25–26). Gideon was talking to God, and God responded with the requested signs, but there were no words from God (6:36–40). This may have simply been a record of Gideon praying. However, the Lord did speak to Gideon in regard to the size of Gideon's army (7:4; 7:7–10). The Lord told Gideon to go against the camp of the enemy, but if he was afraid, he was instructed to go with his servant, and they would hear confirmation of victory from the enemy themselves (7:9–10). Obviously, Gideon was afraid because his servant accompanied him. They heard two of the men speaking, one sharing a dream and the other interpreting it to be their defeat and Gideon's victory. The dream was from God and served as confirmation to Gideon. When he heard the men speaking, he worshipped the Lord (7:13–16).

The angel of the Lord appeared to Manoah's wife to tell her that she was going to have a son and instructed her that her son would be a Nazarite from birth and that he would "begin to save Israel from the hand of the Philistines" (Judg. 13:5). Manoah's wife told her husband of the visitor, calling him "a man of God" and that he had "the appearance of the angel of God, very awesome" (13:6). Manoah prayed to the Lord, asking that the "man of God" would return to teach them what to do with the child to be born. God listened and sent the "angel of God" to the woman while she was in the field. She ran to get her husband, and he came quickly and asked the angel if he was the original messenger. Verse 15 calls this "angel of God," "the angel of the Lord," though at this time Manoah did not know this to be the angel of the Lord (v. 16). Manoah asked the angel's name, and the rather odd answer was given:

> "Why do you ask my name, seeing it is wonder-
> ful?" When the flame went up toward heaven
> from the altar, the angel of the Lord went up
> in the flame of the altar…the angel of the Lord
> appeared no more to Manoah and to his wife.
> (18, 20–21).

Manoah's response was, "We shall surely die for we have seen God" (v. 22).

As Samson grew, the scripture says, "The Spirit of the Lord began to stir him" (v. 25). Nothing more is said to explain or expand the statement. There were several examples of the Spirit of the Lord rushing upon Samson, but there was nothing said about the Lord speaking to him.

Judges 17–18 record the account of Micah who had hired an out-of-work Levite to be his personal priest. Five Danites were sent on a mission to find a place of inheritance. When these spies came to the house of Micah, they recognized the voice of the Levite. They asked him to inquire of the Lord if their journey would succeed. He told them to go in peace, supposedly receiving this revelation from the Lord, though later he would take household idols and become the hired priest of the Danites! It is probable this Levite did not hear from God.

The final account of God speaking in the book of Judges came when certain Israelites went to Bethel to inquire of God to determine who would be first to go against the tribe of Benjamin (20:18 ff.). We are told that the Lord answered, but we are not told how they inquired of Him or how He answered.

Drawing toward the close of the time of the judges, God spoke words of judgment through an unidentified prophet, "Thus the Lord has said" (1 Sam. 2:27). Because of Eli's sons' self-serving use of the sacrifices that had been offered by the people, and the disdain brought on the Lord by them, and by Eli's support of them, this prophet spoke God's warning to Eli.

> The only one of you whom I shall not cut off from my altar shall be spared to weep his eyes out to grieve his heart, and all the descendants of your house shall die by the sword of men. And this that shall come upon your two sons, Hophni and Phinehas, shall be the sign to you: both of them shall die on the same day. And I will raise up for myself a faithful priest, who shall do according to what is in my heart and in my mind. And I will build him a sure house, and he shall go in and out before my anointed forever. (2:33–35)

The warning from the unidentified prophet was magnified by the fact that "the word of the Lord was rare in those days; there was no frequent vision" (1 Sam. 3:2), but "Then the Lord called Samuel" (3:4). This could have been an audible voice, but there is no indication that it was heard by Eli. We are told that "Samuel did not yet know the Lord, and the word of the Lord had not yet been revealed to him" (3:7). The Lord called to Samuel three times, and each time Samuel went to Eli assuming Eli had called him. Finally, "Eli perceived that the Lord was calling the young man." He instructed Samuel to go back to bed, and if he was called again, he was to answer, "Speak, for your servant hears" (3:8–9). "The Lord came and stood, calling as at other times, 'Samuel! Samuel!'" Judgment would come because Eli's sons were blaspheming God, and Eli had done nothing to restrain them. The text says, "Samuel was afraid to tell the vision to Eli." When Eli encouraged Samuel to communicate what he had heard, Samuel told him everything. It was not long before

> All Israel…knew that Samuel was established as a prophet of the Lord. The Lord appeared again at Shiloh, for the Lord revealed himself to Samuel, at Shiloh by the word of the Lord. (3:20–21)

Was this a pre-incarnate appearance of Jesus? Was the revealing of God through a spoken word that Samuel heard? It is impossible to draw a certain conclusion.

Years later, as the Israelites dealt with the nations surrounding them, and as they considered the age of Samuel and the compromised character of his sons, they began to clamor for a king. Samuel brought the matter to the Lord, and the Lord answered,

> Obey the voice of the people in all that they say to you, for they have not rejected you, but they have rejected me from being king over them. According to all the deeds that they have done, from the day I brought them up out of Egypt even to this day, forsaking me and serving other gods, so they are also doing to you. Now then, obey their voice; only you shall solemnly warn them and show them the ways of the king who shall reign over them. (8:7–9)

Additional information was given to the people with the introduction, "So Samuel told all the words of the Lord to the people" (8:10–18). Samuel made his best case against Israel choosing a king, but the people demanded it, and the Lord once again told Samuel to obey the voice of the people in spite of what would happen. How the Lord spoke to Samuel is not indicated.

The Lord had revealed to Samuel the time and place and person that Samuel was to anoint as king of Israel (1 Sam. 9:15 ff.). When Samuel saw Saul, the Lord told Samuel that he was the man to be made king. During the brief conversation, Samuel told Saul that he would make known to him the word of the Lord. Samuel gave Saul a series of commands regarding places where he was to go and people he would meet, and how he was to respond. Samuel also said,

> You will meet a group of prophets coming down from the high place with harp, tambourine, flute, and lyre before them, prophesying. Then

> the Spirit of the LORD will rush upon you, and
> you will prophesy with them and be turned into
> another man. Now when these signs meet you,
> do what your hand finds to do, for God is with
> you. (10:5–8)

As Saul was leaving Samuel, this happened as prophesied.

> When he turned his back to leave Samuel, God
> gave him another heart. And all these signs came
> to pass that day. When they came to Gibeah,
> behold, a group of prophets met him, and the
> Spirit of God rushed upon him, and he proph-
> esied among them. And when all who knew
> him previously saw how he prophesied with the
> prophets, the people said to one another, "What
> has come over the son of Kish? Is Saul also among
> the prophets?" (10:9–11).

While Samuel was at Mizpah (10:17–19), he called the people together to relay what the Lord had communicated to him regarding a king. Lots were cast among the tribes and clans, and the lot fell to Saul, but he was nowhere to be found. He was hiding among the baggage, and it was necessary for the Lord to reveal that (10:22)! When Samuel told the people of the king's rights and duties, he presumably had been given this from the Lord. Samuel recorded it in a book "and laid it up before the Lord" (10:25). This may have been the revelation previously given to Moses recorded in Deuteronomy 17:14–20.

Urim and Thummim were used to discern the Lord's will. They were used by Saul as he inquired of the Lord (14:41–42). Urim and Thummim seemed to be a way to receive a "yes" or "no" answer from God.

> Therefore Saul said, "O LORD God of Israel, why
> have you not answered your servant this day?

If this guilt is in me or in Jonathan my son, O LORD, God of Israel, give Urim. But if this guilt is in your people Israel, give Thummim." And Jonathan and Saul were taken, but the people escaped. Then Saul said, "Cast the lot between me and my son Jonathan." And Jonathan was taken.

Words of the Lord were given to Samuel regarding the end to Saul's reign as king (15:1–3). God chose to speak to Saul through the prophet Samuel. There is no record of any direct revelation from God to the king. Saul and the armies of Israel had been commanded to strike Amalek, sparing nothing, but Saul disobeyed the directives of God he had received from the prophet Samuel. The Lord came to Samuel and said,

"I regret that I have made Saul king, for he has turned back from following me and has not performed my commandments." And Samuel was angry, and he cried to the LORD all night. (15:10–11)

The next morning Saul set up a monument to himself and then met Samuel. He was proudly declaring his obedience, when Samuel challenged his failure to obey. Though Saul finally admitted his sin and asked to be pardoned (15:24–25), Samuel made it clear that Saul had rejected the word of the Lord, and he described what the consequences of that rejection would be: "The LORD has torn the kingdom of Israel from you this day and has given it to a neighbor of yours, who is better than you" (v. 28).

The Lord spoke to Samuel concerning the choosing of David as the next king (16:1–2, 7, 12). While Samuel was reviewing the first son of Jesse, the Lord spoke to him:

Do not look on his appearance or on the height of his stature, because I have rejected him. For

> the LORD sees not as man sees: man looks on the
> outward appearance, but the LORD looks on the
> heart. (1 Sam. 16:7)

When the last son was brought forth, again the Lord spoke to Samuel:

> And the LORD said, "Arise, anoint him, for this
> is he." Then Samuel took the horn of oil and
> anointed him in the midst of his brothers. And
> the Spirit of the LORD rushed upon David from
> that day forward. (16:12–13)

Whatever that means, when David was confessing his sin in Psalm 32 and asking the Lord not to take the Holy Spirit from him, he was likely making a mental reference to this event. It appears that the Lord spoke to Samuel in his spirit or mind rather than in an audible voice or in some physical appearance.

6

God Speaks to the Kings

While David was fleeing from Saul (1 Sam. 23), he was made aware that Keilah was being attacked by the Philistines; he inquired of the Lord if he should attack the Philistine army. This is the first recorded revelation from the Lord to David. The text does not tell us how David inquired or how God answered, but God did answer, telling David to attack. David inquired again, and this time the Lord told him that He would give the Philistines into David's hands. Abiathar, the priest, had fled to Keilah to join David, and he brought with him an ephod. David asked for the ephod, using that to get an answer from the Lord as to whether Saul would come after him, and if Saul did pursue him, would the city of Keilah give him up to Saul. An ephod was a priestly garment, a breastplate containing onyx stones engraved with the names of the twelve tribes of Israel. This breast-plate also contained the sacred lots of Urim and Thummim.

Saul also attempted to receive revelation from the Lord in regard to the Philistines. "And when Saul inquired of the LORD, the LORD did not answer him, either by dreams, or by Urim, or by prophets" (28:6). Desperate, Saul turned to a medium, and he heard from the deceased prophet, Samuel. From the place of departed spirits, Samuel spoke prophetically concerning the final days of Saul's career as king. Samuel spoke the same words here (28:17), as he did to Saul earlier (15:28). Samuel also told Saul that the king and his sons would die at the hands of the Philistines the very next day. Here, God's revelation came from a deceased prophet/judge who spoke to a king who had attempted to contact the dead through a medium! There was an interesting track for divine revelation!

The Amalekites (1 Sam. 30) had attacked the city of Ziklag where the wives and families of David and his men had been living. The city had been burned, but the people had been spared and were taken captive. David called Abiathar the priest to bring the ephod and inquire of the Lord if he should pursue the Amalekites. He was given confirmation. It is important to note that the use of lots were not in the hands of the people but were special "tools" in the hands of the priest to be used by the king to discern direction from the Lord regarding national concerns. When the writer of the Proverbs said, "The lot is cast into the lap, but its every decision is from the Lord" (Prov. 16:33), the author, King Solomon, may well have had Urim and Thummim in mind.

David heard from the Lord concerning his anointing as king over Judah. David also inquired of the Lord concerning his various military pursuits. The people reminded David what the Lord had said to him earlier:

> In times past, when Saul was king over us, it was you who led out and brought in Israel. And the LORD said to you, "You shall be shepherd of my people Israel, and you shall be prince over Israel." So all the elders of Israel came to the king at Hebron, and King David made a covenant with them at Hebron before the LORD, and they anointed David king over Israel. (2 Sam. 5:2–3)

David inquired of the Lord (5:19) that if he should go against the Philistines, would he be successful? He was told to go. Sometime later, he inquired again and was given a specific strategy for victory (5:23–24).

In 2 Samuel 7, the Word of the Lord came to David through the prophet Nathan concerning the building of a temple. God was speaking to His prophet in the night. The temple was not to be built by David but by David's son after his death (vv. 12–13). "In accordance with all this vision, Nathan spoke to David" (7:17). David accepted this word coming through Nathan as from the Lord. David's prayer to the Lord makes this clear (vv. 18–29).

With regard to a totally different matter, the Lord again came to David through the prophet Nathan.

> The Lord sent Nathan to David… "You are the man! Thus says the Lord, the God of Israel…why have you despised the word of the Lord?" (2 Sam. 12:1 ff.)

The judgments against David and his family for his sins against Bathsheba and Uriah were severe. "The child who is born to you will die." After the death of the baby, God, again, through the prophet Nathan, gave the name of David's son who would become the heir to the throne (2 Sam. 12:24–25 and 1 Chron. 28:2–9). Though Nathan brought the word from the Lord, David identified the prophet's words as God speaking directly to him.

As David fled from Absalom, he asked counsel from the priest Zadok, "Are you not a seer?" (2 Sam. 15:27 ff.). David instructed him to return to the city, and he would wait "until word comes from you to inform me." David may have been waiting for God to speak to Zadok so that Zadok could relay the message. He could also have just been waiting for information using Zadok and Abiathar as insiders or spies.

Toward the end of David's reign, the king failed to be submissive to God's Word. This was, surprisingly enough, pointed out by Joab (1 Chron. 21:1 ff.)! This "written word" from God to which Joab was referring was every bit as important as any dream, vision, or audible voice. Note that the Lord spoke to David through the seer (prophet) Gad (21:9 ff.):

> Go and say to David, "Thus says the Lord."

> The angel of the Lord had commanded Gad to say to David. (21:18)

This time David obeyed. In verse 27, the Lord (God) was speaking to the angel of the Lord, presumably, the pre-incarnate second person of the Triune God (compare 21:15–16 with 21:27)!

Consider the following passages from Psalms (1; 2:7 ff.; 12:6; 19:6–14; 25:14; 29; 33:4; 34:4,17; 62:11–12; 65:5; 89:19 ff.; 110; 119). It is important for us to remember that all of the psalms are the written Word of God! As these songs came to David and the other psalmists, clearly God was directing the songs they were writing, though the human authors may not have realized at the time of writing that these songs were revelation from God coming through them.

Prior to his death, David made it clear to his son, Solomon, that the written revelation of the Law of Moses was the word of God (1 Kings 2:2–3). These were God's statutes, God's commandments, God's rules, and God's testimonies, "as it is written in the Law of Moses." Solomon, however, failed to heed many of the laws God had given. Early in his reign, he made marriage alliances with Israel's enemies. In 1 Kings 3, we are told,

> Solomon loved the LORD, walking in the statutes of David his father, only he sacrificed and made offerings at the high places. And the king went to Gibeon to sacrifice there, for that was the great high place. Solomon used to offer a thousand burnt offerings on that altar. At Gibeon the LORD appeared to Solomon in a dream by night, and God said, "Ask what I shall give you."

As Solomon continued to dream, God continued to speak (vv. 11–14). In the dream, Solomon asked,

> Give your servant therefore an understanding mind to govern your people, that I may discern between good and evil, for who is able to govern this your great people? (1 Kings 3:9)

When Solomon woke up, he knew it was a dream (v. 15), but he also knew that the Lord had indeed answered.

Through the wisdom Solomon had been granted,

> He also spoke 3,000 proverbs, and his songs were 1,005. He spoke of trees, from the cedar that is in Lebanon to the hyssop that grows out of the wall. He spoke also of beasts, and of birds, and of reptiles, and of fish. And people of all nations came to hear the wisdom of Solomon, and from all the kings of the earth, who had heard of his wisdom. (4:32–34)

Apparently, some of those proverbs were recorded and are contained in the canonical book we know by that name.

As the temple was being constructed,

> The word of the LORD came to Solomon, "Concerning this house that you are building, if you will walk in my statutes and obey my rules and keep all my commandments and walk in them, then I will establish my word with you, which I spoke to David your father. And I will dwell among the children of Israel and will not forsake my people Israel." (1 Kings 6:11–13)

When the temple was completed and Solomon was giving the dedicatory prayer (1 Kings 8), much of his prayer included words that Moses had recorded in the Law (2 Chron. 7:12 ff.).

God appeared to Solomon a second time. The text says, "as he had appeared at Gibeon" (9:2), which may suggest that this appearance was also in the form of a dream. The Lord acknowledged hearing Solomon's prayer (1 Kings 9), and He made a promise:

> I have consecrated this house that you have built,
> by putting my name there forever. My eyes and
> my heart will be there for all time. (1 Kings 9:3)

However, that promise came with a condition of obedience. The Lord made known His anger toward Solomon for multiplying foreign wives. Because of Solomon's disobedience and accommodation to these foreign wives, many of the Israelites went after other gods (11:9). Twice before, God had appeared to Solomon "concerning this thing." Similar language is used of Solomon that was used against Saul—"I will surely tear the kingdom from you and will give it to your servant" (11:11). Because of David, however, it would not be torn from Solomon but from his son after Solomon's death (11:12).

Though there are no "thus says the Lord" statements in the writings of Solomon (Song of Songs, Proverbs, and Ecclesiastes), Solomon did remind his readers that knowledge and wisdom come from the mouth of the Lord (Prov. 2:6). Solomon also gave examples of what the Lord desires and hates (such as Prov. 11:1; 6:16–19; 15:8–9). Even though Ecclesiastes has no direct reference to a speaking God, we accept the book as being the very words of God to us as they came through a tired and sin-laden king, assuming that this was written toward the end of Solomon's life after his compromises with the multiplication of wives and the worship of their gods. The same could be said concerning Solomon's Song of Songs. There is no mention of God speaking, and yet as a canonical book, this was God's revelation to us through King Solomon.

Not only did God speak to His chosen king, Solomon, but He also spoke to Jeroboam through the prophet Ahijah concerning the division of kingdom.

> And at that time, when Jeroboam went out of
> Jerusalem, the prophet Ahijah the Shilonite
> found him on the road. Now Ahijah had dressed

himself in a new garment, and the two of them were alone in the open country. Then Ahijah laid hold of the new garment that was on him and tore it into twelve pieces. And he said to Jeroboam, "Take for yourself ten pieces, for thus says the LORD, the God of Israel, 'Behold, I am about to tear the kingdom from the hand of Solomon and will give you ten tribes.'" (11:29–31)

As we continue to see, throughout the OT, God chose to speak through His prophets.

An unnamed man of God appeared in 1 Kings 13.

And behold, a man of God came out of Judah by the word of the LORD to Bethel. Jeroboam was standing by the altar to make offerings. And the man cried against the altar by the word of the LORD and said, "O altar, altar, thus says the LORD: 'Behold, a son shall be born to the house of David, Josiah by name, and he shall sacrifice on you the priests of the high places who make offerings on you, and human bones shall be burned on you.'" And he gave a sign the same day, saying, "This is the sign that the LORD has spoken: 'Behold, the altar shall be torn down, and the ashes that are on it shall be poured out.'" (vv. 1–3)

The verses immediately following confirmed this word as from the Lord. Jeroboam, now with a withered hand, pleaded to the unnamed prophet to entreat the Lord for healing. He did, and Jeroboam was healed. Jeroboam invited the prophet to come to his home as a reward, but the prophet refused, having been commanded by the Lord to neither eat or drink nor return home by the same route he had come.

An old prophet who lived in Bethel was told about the events involving the unnamed prophet. He saddled his donkey and found the unnamed prophet resting under an oak tree. The old man identified himself also as a prophet and gave a false prophecy, though claiming it to be a word from God given by an angel (v. 18). The message was that the unnamed prophet should return with him to his house for a meal. Convinced that God had altered His original instructions, the unnamed prophet returned with the old prophet, not realizing that the old prophet was lying. As they were eating, the Lord spoke to the old prophet a message for the unnamed prophet regarding his disobedience and the judgment that would come upon him. The prophecy was fulfilled (v. 24). This strange account surely tells us something about the seriousness of the revelation of God and what He has said is not to be ignored or altered, regardless of what others may claim!

We are next introduced to the prophet Ahijah (1 Kings 14:4 ff.). Abijah, who was the son of Jeroboam, fell sick. Jeroboam wanted to know what would happen to his son, so he asked his wife to disguise herself and visit the blind prophet Ahijah, where the king could hopefully receive an answer from God. The Lord spoke to the prophet, revealing to him that Jeroboam's wife was coming to inquire concerning her son who was ill. As she came, pretending to be someone else, Ahijah immediately spoke, "Come in, wife of Jeroboam." He then prophesied concerning Jeroboam and his son (vv. 7–16). After cataloging Jeroboam's sins, the prophet announced from the Lord the judgment against Jeroboam and his household.

> "Anyone belonging to Jeroboam who dies in the city the dogs shall eat, and anyone who dies in the open country the birds of the heavens shall eat, for the LORD has spoken it." Arise therefore, go to your house. When your feet enter the city, the child shall die. And all Israel shall mourn for him and bury him, for he only of Jeroboam shall come to the grave, because in him there is found something pleasing to the LORD, the God

of Israel, in the house of Jeroboam. Moreover, the LORD will raise up for himself a king over Israel who shall cut off the house of Jeroboam today. And henceforth, the LORD will strike Israel as a reed is shaken in the water and root up Israel out of this good land that he gave to their fathers and scatter them beyond the Euphrates, because they have made their Asherim, provoking the LORD to anger. And he will give Israel up because of the sins of Jeroboam, which he sinned and made Israel to sin. (1 Kings 14:11–16)

The prophet Jehu is introduced in 1 Kings 16. The word of the Lord came to Jehu against Baasha (1 Kings 16:1–3). Baasha was the king of the northern kingdom. The prophecy of judgment was similar to that which was pronounced against Jeroboam. "The word of the Lord" (v. 7) announced that judgment would fall upon Baasha, and verses 10–12 describe the fulfillment of the prophecy through the murderous actions of Zimri, who would rule over Israel all of seven days! The reigns of Omri and Ahab would follow, which brings us to the prophetic ministry of Elijah.

Without introduction, the prophet Elijah bursts on the scene. The Lord gave him a personal message to leave the area (17:2 ff.) and hide at the brook Cherith and then, a brief time later, to travel to Zarephath (v. 8). "The word of the Lord came to him" does not indicate the form or manner of the revelation. The message from the Lord was that he had commanded a widow in Zarephath to feed him. When Elijah arrived, the widow was preparing to use the last of her flour and oil to bake a small breadcake for herself and her son, presumably for their final meal. Elijah requested that she first make a cake for him and then he shared the prophecy that during the entire drought period, her jar of flour and her jug of oil would never be empty. It is reasonable to assume that the command of the Lord to the widow was not something of which she was aware. This was the providential working of the Lord, not revelation.

Sometime later, Elijah received a personal message from the Lord to go to King Ahab. "After many days, the word of the Lord came to Elijah, in the third year" (18:1). This may suggest that even to prophets, God's revelation was not as frequent as we might have assumed. The prophecy in chapter 17 was the record of the beginning of the drought. Chapter 18 opens in the third year of the drought with the promise that God was soon going to bring rain. The account of the meeting with Ahab and the contest on Mount Carmel and the answer of God by fire and the sending of rain were all evidences of God's involvement, but there was no recorded revelation from God. Elijah's actions and words were based on God's previous revelation. Following the great victory over the prophets of Baal, Elijah received a message from Queen Jezebel promising to kill the prophet. Elijah made haste, running for his life, first to Beersheba, one hundred twenty miles from Mount Carmel, and then a day's journey further! Elijah, no doubt exhausted, asked the Lord to take his life.

While sleeping, Elijah was visited by the angel of the Lord (19:5–8). The angel twice provided a baked cake of bread and a jar of water and told Elijah to arise and eat. The second time the angel gave the enigmatic message, "For the journey is too great for you." After the angel visits, Elijah traveled for forty more days to Mount Horeb (Sinai).

"The word of the Lord came to him" (19:9) while he was taking refuge in a cave on Mount Horeb. Many have used this text, which speaks of "a still small voice" or a "low whisper" as an example of how God, through His Spirit, speaks to people today, but the text does not say that. The Lord was not in the wind or in the earthquake or in the fire, nor was He in the "low whisper." Verse 13 says, "And behold there came a voice to him." This was the Lord speaking. And He asked the same question in verse 13 following the dramatic demonstrations that He had asked in verse 9 before those demonstrations, "What are you doing here, Elijah?" The Lord redirected Elijah and gave him several assignments, some he fulfilled and others he failed to complete.

Rather than being a proof text for how God speaks to us today, there is a more plausible explanation of the text. Elijah believed he was the only faithful follower of the Lord. After receiving the threat of death from Jezebel, he apparently was determined to go to Mount Horeb, better known as Mount Sinai. In fact, while receiving the food and water from the angel of the Lord in the wilderness, the angel had said, "Arise and eat, for the journey is too great for you." The angel did not tell Elijah to take any journey; that was his decision. He believed he was in a similar situation as was Moses after the people had sinned with the golden calf. Moses had met with the Lord and was exposed to His glory, and he and the people of Israel were more or less given a new start. Elijah apparently believed that the same might happen to him at Mount Sinai. When he arrived, the Lord asked, "What are you doing here, Elijah?" Elijah gave his "woe-is-me," "I've been faithful to you and look where it has gotten me" complaint, and the Lord told him to go out of the cave and stand before the Lord. That's when the demonstrations of power (the wind, the earthquake, and the fire) were given, but the Lord was not in any of them. After the fire came the sound of a low whisper. Though our translations may say "low whisper" or "still small voice," the meaning of the text is more likely describing silence. This was not some soft, quiet communication from God to Elijah. Rather it was more of the calm after the storm. As Elijah emerged from wherever he had sought shelter from the spectacular displays of God's power, the Lord spoke the same question He asked when Elijah arrived at Mount Sinai, "What are you doing here, Elijah?" Elijah gave the same answer he gave the first time that he was asked that question. In other words, nothing had changed. Elijah was told to return to his work as a prophet, and he was given some assignments to complete including the anointing of his replacement. God also made it clear that He had a remnant of faithful followers and He would accomplish His purposes. Rather than this being a text about how God speaks to us in a still small voice, it is a text about God calling His prophet to carry out the mission that God had assigned to him to complete.[7]

[7.] Chaplain Mike (Internet Monk), "Rethinking the Text: God's Still Small Voice?" Online article. This article is worth finding and reading. The commentary above on 1 Kings 19 is in part of summary of the article.

Elijah failed to accomplish all that God had told him to do before He swept him up to heaven in a fiery chariot, but for some time after the Sinai experience, Elijah did continue as a prophet of God. We are told in 1 Kings 21,

> Then the word of the LORD came to Elijah the Tishbite, saying, "Arise, go down to meet Ahab king of Israel, who is in Samaria; behold, he is in the vineyard of Naboth, where he has gone to take possession. And you shall say to him, 'Thus says the LORD, "Have you killed and also taken possession?"' And you shall say to him, 'Thus says the LORD: "In the place where dogs licked up the blood of Naboth shall dogs lick your own blood."'" (1 Kings 21;17–19)

In a somewhat surprising turn of events, the Lord again spoke to Elijah:

> Have you seen how Ahab has humbled himself before me? Because he has humbled himself before me, I will not bring the disaster in his days; but in his son's days I will bring the disaster upon his house. (1 Kings 21:29)

Later in Elijah's ministry, after King Jehoshaphat died, the king's firstborn son, Jehoram, reigned in his place. He walked in the ways of the kings of Israel. In fact, his wife was a daughter of King Ahab and Queen Jezebel! What Jehoshaphat had sought to destroy, his wicked son had restored. His actions prompted a prophetic letter from the prophet Elijah:

> Thus says the LORD, the God of David your father, "Because you have not walked in the ways of Jehoshaphat your father, or in the ways of Asa king of Judah, but have walked in the way of the

kings of Israel and have enticed Judah and the inhabitants of Jerusalem into whoredom, as the house of Ahab led Israel into whoredom, and also you have killed your brothers, of your father's house, who were better than you, behold, the LORD will bring a great plague on your people, your children, your wives, and all your possessions, and you yourself will have a severe sickness with a disease of your bowels, until your bowels come out because of the disease, day by day." (2 Chron. 21:12–15)

God spoke by the prophets in many ways, and what Elijah had written came true!

Toward the end of Elijah's ministry, the angel of the Lord spoke to him in relation to the king of Israel, Ahaziah (2 Kings 1). The king had fallen through a lattice and was injured. He summoned messengers to inquire of the god of Ekron whether or not he would recover. The angel of the Lord spoke to Elijah, ordering him to go to intercept the messengers who had been dispatched to Ekron and ask why they failed to inquire of the Lord—"Is it because there is no God in Israel?" (2 Kings 1:6). Elijah obeyed and gave this word to the messengers to relay to Ahaziah:

Thus says the Lord, "You shall not come down from the bed to which you have gone up, but you shall surely die." (2 Kings 1:6)

The king determined from the messengers' description that the prophecy came from Elijah. From his sickbed, he made attempts to destroy the prophet but failed. "So he died according to the word of the Lord that Elijah had spoken" (2 Kings 1:17).

2 Kings 2 revealed the account of Elijah being taken into heaven. Elijah explained to Elisha where the Lord was sending him, first to Bethel, then to Jericho, and finally to the Jordan (vv. 2, 4, 6). There is no record of how or when those revelations came.

God does not always identify His prophets. Such was the case in a prophecy of victory given to King Ahab against Ben-hadad, king of Syria.

> And behold, a prophet came near to Ahab king of Israel and said, "Thus says the LORD, Have you seen all this great multitude? Behold, I will give it into your hand this day, and you shall know that I am the LORD." And Ahab said, "By whom?" He said, "Thus says the LORD, By the servants of the governors of the districts." Then he said, "Who shall begin the battle?" He answered, "You." (1 Kings 20:13–14)

Israel was victorious, but Ben-hadad escaped. The prophet who had given the word of the Lord about the initial battle gave another message to the king of Israel that Ben-hadad would fight again in the spring. Though there is no direct statement that this was from the Lord, it is reasonable to assume that it was from God (v. 22).

That spring, Ben-hadad came to fight. His army far outnumbered the Israeli army.

> And a man of God came near and said to the king of Israel, "Thus says the LORD, 'Because the Syrians have said, "The LORD is a god of the hills but he is not a god of the valleys," therefore I will give all this great multitude into your hand, and you shall know that I am the LORD.'" (20:28)

One hundred thousand Syrian foot soldiers were struck down in one day! Once again, Ben-hadad escaped and fled to an inner chamber in the city. Hearing and hoping the reports were true that the Israeli kings were merciful, Ben-hadad and his servants put on sackcloth and pleaded for their lives. Ahab not only spared them but declared Ben-hadad to be his brother. He made a covenant with him and let him go.

At the command of the Lord, one of the sons of the prophets gave a descriptive prophetic message:

> And a certain man of the sons of the prophets said to his fellow at the command of the LORD, "Strike me, please." But the man refused to strike him. Then he said to him, "Because you have not obeyed the voice of the LORD, behold, as soon as you have gone from me, a lion shall strike you down." And as soon as he had departed from him, a lion met him and struck him down. Then he found another man and said, "Strike me, please." And the man struck him—struck him and wounded him. So the prophet departed and waited for the king by the way, disguising himself with a bandage over his eyes. And as the king passed, he cried to the king and said, "Your servant went out into the midst of the battle, and behold, a soldier turned and brought a man to me and said, 'Guard this man; if by any means he is missing, your life shall be for his life, or else you shall pay a talent of silver.' And as your servant was busy here and there, he was gone." The king of Israel said to him, "So shall your judgment be; you yourself have decided it." Then he hurried to take the bandage away from his eyes, and the king of Israel recognized him as one of the prophets. And he said to him, "Thus says the LORD, Because you have let go out of your hand the man whom I had devoted to destruction, therefore your life shall be for his life, and your people for his people." And the king of Israel went to his house vexed and sullen and came to Samaria. (20:35–43)

The record of the prophecy given to Rehoboam through the prophet Shemaiah is recorded in 2 Chronicles 12:5–8.

> Then Shemaiah the prophet came to Rehoboam and to the princes of Judah, who had gathered at Jerusalem because of Shishak, and said to them, "Thus says the LORD, 'You abandoned me, so I have abandoned you to the hand of Shishak.'" Then the princes of Israel and the king humbled themselves and said, "The LORD is righteous." When the LORD saw that they humbled themselves, the word of the LORD came to Shemaiah: "They have humbled themselves. I will not destroy them, but I will grant them some deliverance, and my wrath shall not be poured out on Jerusalem by the hand of Shishak. Nevertheless, they shall be servants to him, that they may know my service and the service of the kingdoms of the countries."

As with so many of the prophetic messages, we are not told how they were received, but we are told that they were from the Lord.

The same could be said about the prophet Azariah (2 Chron. 15:1–8). The scripture text says, "The Spirit of God came upon Azariah, the son of Oded." The prophet offered encouragement to King Asa reminding him, "The Lord is with you while you are with him." Asa listened to the prophet and put away his detestable idols. He also deposed his mother because of her idolatry. Other reforms resulted from Asa listening to the words of God.

However, King Asa did not always respond so positively to the word of the Lord! Baasha, the king of Israel, had gone against Judah, so Asa took silver and gold from the treasures in the temple and used them to hire help from Ben-hadad, king of Syria. The seer, Hanani (2 Chron. 16:7), challenged the decision of relying on Syria rather than on the Lord. Asa became angry and had the prophet imprisoned in stocks. He also "inflicted cruelties upon some of the people at the same time" (2 Chron. 16:10). Asa was diseased in his feet, which may or may not have been judgment for his disobedience, but even in the disease he did not seek the Lord.

Perhaps what happened to his father prompted Jehoshaphat, who was now the king of Judah, to encourage the people to "believe in the Lord your God, and you will be established; believe in his prophets and you will succeed" (20:20). The counsel was sound, but it was not always followed. Jehoshaphat joined with the king of Israel, "who acted wickedly," in a ship building enterprise.

> Then Eliezer the son of Dodavahu of Mareshah prophesied against Jehoshaphat, saying, "Because you have joined with Ahaziah, the LORD will destroy what you have made." And the ships were wrecked and were not able to go to Tarshish. (2 Chron. 20:37)

Once again Jehoshaphat visited Ahab, and in the course of conversation, Ahab asked the king of Judah to join him in battle against Syria (1 Kings 22). Perhaps having gained a little wisdom, before entering into a coalition, Jehoshaphat wanted to hear from the prophets what God had to say about it. Ahab called four hundred of his prophets, and they gave the unanimous approval to go against Syria assuring the king of victory! Unconvinced, Jehoshaphat asked if there was at least one man among them who was a prophet of God and not a puppet of the king. Ahab admitted that there was one, Micaiah, but Ahab hated him because he never prophesied anything good for him! But to appease Jehoshaphat, Micaiah was summoned but also warned.

> And the messenger who went to summon Micaiah said to him, "Behold, the words of the prophets with one accord are favorable to the king. Let your word be like the word of one of them and speak favorably." (1 Kings 22:13)

Micaiah mockingly agreed with Ahab's prophets, but it was clear to the king that he was not speaking in the name of the Lord. The exchange that follows is fascinating.

> And Micaiah said, "Therefore hear the word of the LORD: I saw the LORD sitting on his throne, and all the host of heaven standing beside him on his right hand and on his left; and the LORD said, 'Who will entice Ahab, that he may go up and fall at Ramoth-gilead?' And one said one thing, and another said another. Then a spirit came forward and stood before the LORD, saying, 'I will entice him.' And the LORD said to him, 'By what means?' And he said, 'I will go out, and will be a lying spirit in the mouth of all his prophets.' And he said, 'You are to entice him, and you shall succeed; go out and do so.' Now therefore behold, the LORD has put a lying spirit in the mouth of all these your prophets; the LORD has declared disaster for you." Then Zedekiah the son of Chenaanah came near and struck Micaiah on the cheek and said, "How did the Spirit of the LORD go from me to speak to you?" And Micaiah said, "Behold, you shall see on that day when you go into an inner chamber to hide yourself." And the king of Israel said, "Seize Micaiah, and take him back to Amon the governor of the city and to Joash the king's son, and say, 'Thus says the king, "Put this fellow in prison and feed him meager rations of bread and water, until I come in peace."'" And Micaiah said, "If you return in peace, the LORD has not spoken by me." And he said, "Hear, all you peoples!" (1 Kings 22:19–28)

In spite of Micaiah's prophecy, Jehoshaphat joined Ahab, and it nearly cost him his life! Jehoshaphat survived, but Ahab was killed in the battle.

The word of God proclaimed by the true prophets of God was not often well received. We just considered how Micaiah spent significant time in chains. The prophet Zechariah (2 Chron. 24:20 ff.) was stoned to death for speaking the word of God. His death came at the hands of a king of Judah who, for most of his reign, would have been considered a good and even godly king.

> Then the Spirit of God clothed Zechariah the son of Jehoiada the priest, and he stood above the people, and said to them, "Thus says God, 'Why do you break the commandments of the LORD, so that you cannot prosper? Because you have forsaken the LORD, he has forsaken you.'" But they conspired against him, and by command of the king they stoned him with stones in the court of the house of the LORD. Thus Joash the king did not remember the kindness that Jehoiada, Zechariah's father, had shown him, but killed his son. And when he was dying, he said, "May the LORD see and avenge!" (2 Chron. 24:20–22)

God's prophets were often expected to speak God's Word in dangerous situations. Judah had turned from the Lord, and God allowed the northern kingdom of Israel to form a coalition with the Syrians to deliver His judgment against the southern kingdom. The coalition captured two hundred thousand people from Judah and intended to enslave the captives. A prophet named Oded was sent by God to address the Israelites at Samaria concerning their actions. He met the army and delivered this message from the Lord.

> "Behold, because the LORD, the God of your fathers, was angry with Judah, he gave them into your hand, but you have killed them in a

rage that has reached up to heaven. And now you intend to subjugate the people of Judah and Jerusalem, male and female, as your slaves. Have you not sins of your own against the LORD your God? Now hear me and send back the captives from your relatives whom you have taken, for the fierce wrath of the LORD is upon you." (2 Chron. 28:9–11)

The northern kingdom listened to the words of God from the prophet and released the captives.

The OT text does not always tell us the method God used to speak to His people. In 2 Chronicles 33:10, we are told, "The LORD spoke to Manasseh and to his people, but they paid no attention." It is likely that this message came through a prophet. In verse 18, we are told,

Now the rest of the acts of Manasseh, and his prayer to his God, and the words of the seers who spoke to him in the name of the LORD, the God of Israel, behold, they are in the Chronicles of the Kings of Israel.

The mention of "the seers" strongly suggests the prophets' involvement. Because Manasseh would not listen to the Word of the Lord, God allowed him to be captured with hooks and to be bound with chains and brought to Babylon. It was as a humiliated captive that the wicked king called out to God and "humbled himself greatly before the God of his fathers" (2 Chron. 33:12). God heard Manasseh's prayer, and He allowed Manasseh to return to Jerusalem and to his kingdom.

It is important to remember that God's revelation also came to the leaders and to the people through the previously recorded Word of God. During the reign of Josiah, the king was busy with various reforms. Idols and altars were destroyed, and money was collected to make repairs on the house of the Lord. While this was in process, Hilkiah, the priest, found a copy of the book of the Law of Moses. Hilkiah gave the book to secretary, Shaphan, and the secretary brought the book to King Josiah and began to read portions of it to him. When the king heard these words, he tore his clothes in repentance and commanded,

> Go, inquire of the LORD for me and for those who are left in Israel and in Judah, concerning the words of the book that has been found. For great is the wrath of the LORD that is poured out on us, because our fathers have not kept the word of the LORD, to do according to all that is written in this book. (2 Chron. 34:21)

At the king's directive, Hilkiah and others went to the prophetess Huldah, and she said to them,

> Thus says the LORD, the God of Israel: "Tell the man who sent you to me, Thus says the LORD, Behold, I will bring disaster upon this place and upon its inhabitants, all the curses that are written in the book that was read before the king of Judah. Because they have forsaken me and have made offerings to other gods, that they might provoke me to anger with all the works of their hands, therefore my wrath will be poured out on this place and will not be quenched. But to the king of Judah, who sent you to inquire of the LORD, thus shall you say to him, Thus says the LORD, the God of Israel: Regarding the words that you have heard, because your heart was tender and you humbled yourself before God when you heard his words against this place and its inhabitants, and you have humbled yourself before me and have torn your clothes and wept before me, I also have heard you, declares the

LORD. Behold, I will gather you to your fathers, and you shall be gathered to your grave in peace, and your eyes shall not see all the disaster that I will bring upon this place and its inhabitants." (2 Chron. 34:23–28)

The message was taken back to King Josiah. He gathered the elders of Judah and Jerusalem, and they went to the house of the Lord with the men of Judah and the inhabitants of Jerusalem and also the priests and Levites, and the king read to them "all the words of the Book of the Covenant that had been found in the house of the LORD" (2 Chron. 34:30). The king then made a covenant before the Lord to do what the word of the Lord said. He called upon the residents of Jerusalem to make the same covenant. The word of God affected Josiah's rule for the remainder of his life. It is surprising that even the kings of Judah who were considered godly would have had virtually no knowledge of the OT Law! King Josiah appeared to have no prior knowledge to God's revelation until "the book" was found and brought to him and read.

In the final chapter of 2 Chronicles, we are introduced to Cyrus, the king of Persia. The author of 2 Chronicles reminded us that the decree by the Persian king to build the house of the Lord in Jerusalem was the fulfillment of the prophecy made by Jeremiah.

Now in the first year of Cyrus king of Persia, that the word of the LORD by the mouth of Jeremiah might be fulfilled, the LORD stirred up the spirit of Cyrus king of Persia, so that he made a procla-mation throughout all his kingdom and also put it in writing: "Thus says Cyrus king of Persia, 'The LORD, the God of heaven, has given me all the kingdoms of the earth, and he has charged me to build him a house at Jerusalem, which is in Judah. Whoever is among you of all his people, may the LORD his God be with him. Let him go up.'" (2 Chron. 36:22–23)

God Speaks through the Canonical Prophets

We move now from the kings to the canonical prophets, the major and minor prophetic books of the OT—Isaiah through Malachi—to discover how God spoke through them. We begin with Jonah who prophesied about 770 BC. He, along with the prophets Amos (about 760 BC) and Hosea (about 730 BC), was prophesying to the northern kingdom after the time of Elijah and Elisha, prior to the time when the northern kingdom was destroyed by the Assyrians in 722 BC.

"The word of the Lord came to Jonah" (1:1 ff.). Jonah was told to go to Nineveh, the capital city of the Assyrian Empire, to call out judgment against the Ninevites. For numerous reasons, Jonah disobeyed and headed in the opposite direction. He managed to secure passage on a ship headed to Tarsus, and all seemed to be well until God caused a great storm resulting in Jonah being thrown overboard. This was not the first time a prophet failed to do what God told him to do, resulting in God's discipline. This account is more about the prophet Jonah than any prophecy given by Jonah. The only prophecy declared by him is recorded is 3:4, "Jonah began to go into the city, going a day's journey. And he called out, 'Yet forty days, and Nineveh shall be overthrown!'"

After Jonah was thrown into the sea and swallowed by a great fish, he prayed to the Lord. "And the LORD spoke to the fish, and it vomited Jonah out upon the dry land" (Jon. 2:10). As the sovereign God over all of His creation, God directed the fish to take Jonah a little closer to his assigned destination! It is likely that Jonah's original commission was by vision. The Lord speaking to the fish provides the reminder that He controls all of His creation. When He makes known His will to His nonhuman creation, they respond in obedience. How His will was communicated to His nonhuman creation, we are not told.

Following Jonah's repentance, God spoke to His prophet a second time, "Arise, go to Nineveh, that great city, and call against it the message that I tell you." We are not told how the message came to Jonah, but the words that he spoke to the people of Nineveh were certainly received as from the Lord God. "And the people of Nineveh believed God" (3:5). From what we read in chapter 4, it is hard to imagine that Jonah's message of warning and doom was delivered with persuasive passion! Nevertheless, according to Jesus,

> The men of Nineveh will rise up at the judgment with this generation and condemn it, for they repented at the preaching of Jonah, and behold, something greater than Jonah is here. (Matt. 12:41)

Clearly, Jonah wanted the Ninevites to be destroyed, but he delivered the message God told him to give. When God spared the city, Jonah asked God to take his life! After a series of illustrations involving a plant and a worm and a scorching wind, there was an extended conversation between God and Jonah, though it was unclear in what form this occurred (4:4, 8–11). Much of the conversation from the Lord involved questions concerning the right that Jonah had to be angry and bigoted toward the Ninevites and God's right to extend His pity on the wicked city following their repentance.

The prophet Amos was from the southern kingdom, but his prophecy was directed against the northern kingdom. In verse 3 of the first chapter, the prophet wrote, "Thus says the Lord." Amos relayed to the people what God had made known to Him earlier. The Lord, through the prophet, had messages of judgment for several cities and nations including Damascus (1:3–5), Gaza (1:6–8), Tyre (1:9–10), Edom (1:11–12), the Ammonites (1:13–15), Moab

(2:1–3), Judah (2:4–5), and Israel (2:6–16). Each of these prophetic announcements of judgment began with, "Thus says the LORD."

Amos had stern words for the northern kingdom, "Hear this word that the Lord has spoken against you, O people of Israel." The recipients of the warnings were further identified "against the whole family that I brought out of Egypt." It is interesting to note what Amos recorded in regard to the role of the prophet in God's revelation to His people throughout the OT: "For the Lord GOD does nothing without revealing his secret to his servants the prophets" (3:7). The point of the passage seemed to be that God would send disaster as He wills on those who certainly deserve it, but as a God of grace, He would not send that disaster without a warning, and His warning would come through the message He would give to His prophets to communicate to His people.

As we might expect, this prophetic book is filled with messages from the Lord: "Therefore thus says the Lord God" (3:11), and "Thus says the Lord" (3:12), and "declares the Lord (3:13, 15). The same is true in chapters 4–6 with, "Declares the Lord," "the Lord God Almighty says," "Thus says the Lord God," etc. In chapter 7, Amos told his readers, "This is what the Lord God showed me" (7:1). Amos did not explain how the Lord showed him, but there was an ongoing conversation with the Lord throughout chapter 7.

Amos endured challenges concerning his ministry. For example, Amaziah, the priest at Bethel, was not happy with the prophecies Amos announced. The priest told Amos,

> O seer, go, flee away to the land of Judah, and eat bread there, and prophesy there, but never again prophesy at Bethel, for it is the king's sanctuary, and it is a temple of the kingdom. (7:12–13)

Amos answered,

> I was no prophet, nor a prophet's son, but I was a herdsman and a dresser of sycamore figs. But the LORD took me from following the flock, and

the LORD said to me, "Go, prophesy to my people Israel." Now therefore hear the word of the
LORD. "You say, 'Do not prophesy against Israel,
and do not preach against the house of Isaac.'
Therefore, thus says the LORD." (7:14–17)

Nearly the entire content of this book is a prophetic statement
from the Lord. This is in contrast with what we have seen previously in prophetic utterances. In several other books of prophecy,
there were brief statements from the Lord. Here, entire prophetic
announcements and judgments were given by the Lord, which Amos
merely recorded. His prophecy ended with God's promise to restore
His people.

"I will restore the fortunes of my people Israel,
and they shall rebuild the ruined cities and
inhabit them; they shall plant vineyards and
drink their wine, and they shall make gardens
and eat their fruit. I will plant them on their land,
and they shall never again be uprooted out of the
land that I have given them," says the LORD your
God. (9:14–15)

Hosea began his prophetic book with a declaration that the
word of the Lord came to him: "When the Lord first spoke through
Hosea, the Lord said to Hosea" (1:2). This, along with chapter 3, was
a personal prophecy to illustrate a prophetic message to the people of
Israel. Hosea was instructed by the Lord to take a prostitute as a wife.
Three children were born from this union, and the Lord instructed
Hosea what to name his two sons and one daughter.

Chapters 2 and 4 are declarations from the Lord concerning
sins of Israel and the judgment to come upon the nation. Hosea's
personal life was used as an illustration to the people of the northern
kingdom. Chapters 5–14 form a long prophetic message against the
house of Israel. Statements such as "declares the Lord" and "the Lord
said to me" (2:16; 3:1) remind us that God had spoken to Hosea,

and Hosea made known to his readers that he was recording what the Lord had said to him, "Hear the word of the Lord" (4:1), "Hear this, O priests" (5:1).

The prophecy from God to Obadiah (840 BC) came in the form of a *vision* (v. 1). This entire book is a prophecy of God against the Edomites, delivered from this otherwise unknown prophet as he relayed the message he had received in this vision. The message was one of judgment against the people of Edom: "Thus says the Lord God concerning Edom" (v. 1). Edom was famous for her capital city, Petra, the city carved out of sandstone. The people of Edom believed themselves to be safe in the rocks. They grew proud and arrogant in their position. Arab invaders drove the Edomites from their strongholds. By the time of Jesus, Edom no longer existed as a nation and by AD 70, Edom had completely disappeared.

The time of the prophet Joel is uncertain. If Joel lived in the 800 BC, his prophecy could have been written about the time when the boy-king Joash was crowned king of Judah (2 Kings 8–11). The method God used to bring "The word of the Lord that came to Joel" was not given. The Lord warned His prophet about a coming locust invasion (1:4 ff.; 2:4 ff.), which was used as an illustration of the coming "day of the Lord" (1:15; 2:11). There was also revelation concerning a promised restoration of God's people (2:18 ff.). Of interest to us in this study is the promise Joel received from the Lord regarding the outpouring of God's Spirit.

> And it shall come to pass afterward, that I will pour out my Spirit on all flesh; your sons and your daughters shall prophesy, your old men shall dream dreams, and your young men shall see visions. Even on the male and female servants in those days I will pour out my Spirit. And I will show wonders in the heavens and on the earth, blood and fire and columns of smoke. The sun shall be turned to darkness, and the moon to blood, before the great and awesome day of the LORD comes. And it shall come to pass that every-

ONE who calls on the name of the LORD shall be
saved. For in Mount Zion and in Jerusalem there
shall be those who escape, as the LORD has said,
and among the survivors shall be those whom the
LORD calls. (2:28–32)

Was all or part of this fulfilled on the day of Pentecost following
the Lord's ascension? This is an important text to our discussion, for
it speaks of revelation in the form of dreams and visions that were to
occur "afterward." Peter quoted this passage in Acts 2, so that must
be taken into consideration. It seems that parts of this, at least, have
a future fulfillment at the end of the age (vv. 31–32), but the pour-
ing out of the Spirit seems to have been fulfilled at Pentecost. What
happened in Acts 2 was the beginning of something new. The Holy
Spirit was actively involved in the lives of individuals—"I will pour
out my Spirit on all flesh; your sons and your daughters shall prophesy." Prophesying was the proclamation of God's truth concerning
the Lord Jesus Christ. That's what Peter did in Acts 2. There were
certainly some dreams and visions recorded in the NT experienced
by Paul, Peter, Stephen, and John and some prophesying (Philip's
four unmarried daughters, Agabus, as well as the NT writers). Does
the fulfillment or partial fulfillment of Joel 2 open the door for personal prophecy, for God speaking directly to individual believers
today apart from His written Word? As we work our way into the
NT, hopefully we will be able to answer that question based on the
Scripture itself.

Joel also recorded the promise of a future judgment of the
nations (3:1 ff.). It would be instructive to compare chapter 3 with
Revelation 19. This entire book is one prophetic statement from
God to the nation of Israel. There is no interaction with the prophet.

We turn our attention now to the contemporary prophets,
Isaiah and Micah, who prophesied about 700 BC. Isaiah is a lengthy
prophecy with extended messages from the Lord to Judah as well
as to other nations. These messages were given to Isaiah to record
and communicate. As has been considered, the prophets had the
most extensive recorded utterances from God to this point in our

study. There are sections of historical information such as in chapters 36–37, but the majority of Isaiah is a prophetic message from God. "The vision of Isaiah the son of Amoz, which he saw concerning Judah and Jerusalem" (v. 1). "For the Lord has spoken" (1:2). "Hear the word of the Lord" (1:10), "says the Lord" (1:11), "the mouth of the Lord has spoken (1:20), "the Lord declares" (1:24), etc. These continue throughout the prophecy. A few examples will illustrate.

"In the year that King Uzziah died, I saw the Lord sitting upon a throne…and I heard the voice of the Lord saying" (6:1, 8). Notice the conversation that took place in chapter 6. There were a number of times when the Lord spoke clearly, presumably through Isaiah, but that was not stated. For example,

> I am the Lord; that is my name; my glory I give
> to no other, nor my praise to carved idols. Behold
> the former things have come to pass, and new
> things I now declare; before they spring forth I
> tell you of them. (Isa. 42:8–9)

Chapter 7 is an important section for our consideration. "And the Lord said to Isaiah" (7:3). Notice that the Lord was speaking to Isaiah, telling him to speak to King Ahaz, "say to him" (v. 4), "Thus says the Lord God" (v. 7), and, "Again the Lord spoke to Ahaz" (v. 10). This is not God speaking directly to King Ahaz, but it is God speaking through the prophet Isaiah. When the prophet Isaiah spoke to Ahaz, it was God speaking through him. Consider verses 12–14:

> But Ahaz said, "I will not ask, and I will not put
> the LORD to the test." And he [presumably Isaiah]
> said, "Hear then, O house of David! Is it too little
> for you to weary men, that you weary my God
> also? Therefore the Lord himself will give you a
> sign."
> Then the Lord said to me… The Lord spoke
> to me again…spoke thus to me. (8:1, 5, 11)

This is fairly consistent throughout the book. Isaiah summarized the pattern, "At that time, the Lord spoke by Isaiah" (20:2). Surely, by now, the pattern has been established that God gave His OT revelation through the prophets!

Some of Isaiah's prophecies were given as oracles from God. An oracle was a message from God. In 13:1, Isaiah described such a message as, "An oracle concerning Babylon which Isaiah the son of Amoz saw." There are several examples of these in Isaiah's prophecy (14:28; 15:1; 17:1; 19:1; 21:1, 11, 13; 22:1; 23:1). Other prophecies were revelations of what God said about Himself. There is an example of this in chapter 25. The chapter begins with Isaiah's praise to the Lord (vv. 1–5), and then Isaiah expressed what the Lord would do (vv. 6–12). In chapters 37–38, we get a glimpse of Hezekiah as he was threatened by the king of Assyria. He prayed to the Lord, and Isaiah brought the answer from God to him (37:21–35). The same is true in chapter 38.

Isaiah's prophecy appears to be, at least for the most part, the record of a vision he was given from God. The vision would cover the immediate matters of the impending judgment against the northern kingdom, the judgment to come against Judah, which would occur more than one hundred years later, and judgments against various nations. Isaiah also prophesied the coming of the promised Messiah (Isa. 7, 9), the death of the Messiah (53), the return of the Lord in power and glory, and the restoration of all things (60–66). Isaiah saw these things in a vision and wrote about them as directed by the Spirit of God.

Micah, a contemporary of Isaiah, also received a vision from God, and his prophecy was the record of that vision. His prophecy began, "The word of the Lord that came to Micah...which he saw concerning Samaria and Jerusalem" (1:1). The things that Micah "saw" were future events.

Nahum's prophecy was directed against the Assyrian Empire. One hundred fifty years earlier, God had extended His mercy to the city of Nineveh through the preaching of the prophet Jonah. There would be no more mercy for Nineveh. The message of the prophecy was that Nineveh would fall, and that the fall would be great, and that the city and empire deserved to fall.

The prophecy came as "an oracle concerning Nineveh. The book of the vision of Nahum." The entire book is this oracle without any interaction between the author and the Lord. The first eleven verses of the prophecy speak of God's wrath against Nineveh. In verses 12–13, "Thus says the Lord" was a message to Judah. Then verse 14 returns to judgment against Nineveh, specifically to the Assyrian king. Verse 15 returns to Judah. Chapter 2 addressed the destruction of Nineveh.

> Behold, I am against you, declares the LORD of hosts, and I will burn your chariots in smoke, and the sword shall devour your young lions. I will cut off your prey from the earth, and the voice of your messengers shall no longer be heard. (v. 13)

The prophecy ends with,

> Your shepherds are asleep, O king of Assyria; your nobles slumber. Your people are scattered on the mountains with none to gather them. There is no easing your hurt; your wound is grievous. All who hear the news about you clap their hands over you. For upon whom has not come your unceasing evil? (2:18–19)

Daniel's prophecy begins just prior to the Babylonian captivity. Daniel had been taken captive and transported to Babylon as one of the young men who would be brainwashed and trained to serve in the Babylonian empire. We are introduced to the prophetic ministry of Daniel in chapter 2. Daniel asked God for revelation realizing that the king had already determined to kill all the wise men, including Daniel and his friends. He sought the prayer support of his friends.

> Then Daniel went to his house and made the matter known to Hananiah, Mishael, and Azariah, his companions, and told them to seek mercy from the God of heaven concerning this mystery, so that Daniel and his companions might not be destroyed with the rest of the wise men of Babylon. (2:17–18)

During the night, in a vision, the dream of Nebuchadnezzar was revealed and explained (2:19). Daniel concluded the experience with a psalm of praise (2:19–23).

Daniel came before the king.

> The king declared to Daniel, whose name was Belteshazzar, "Are you able to make known to me the dream that I have seen and its interpretation?" Daniel answered the king and said, "No wise men, enchanters, magicians, or astrologers can show to the king the mystery that the king has asked, but there is a God in heaven who reveals mysteries, and he has made known to King Nebuchadnezzar what will be in the latter days." (2:26–28)

The revelation and interpretation were then given (2:29–45).

In chapter 3, a different aspect of God's revelatory work is evident, though more assumed than stated. God was speaking to Daniel's three friends. There appeared to be some conversation in the fiery furnace as the four of them walked in the fire chamber, though only three had been thrown into the furnace. Daniel suggested the identity of the fourth man in the fire in the king's own response to his question:

> Did we not cast three men bound into the fire…
> but I see four men unbound, walking in the
> midst of the fire, and they are not hurt; and the
> appearance of the fourth is like a son of the gods.
> (3:24–25)

The identity of the fourth man in the fire could have been the angel of the Lord. From where did the resolve to obey God and not men come prior to this?

> Shadrach, Meshach, and Abednego answered and
> said to the king, "O Nebuchadnezzar, we have no
> need to answer you in this matter. If this be so,
> our God whom we serve is able to deliver us from
> the burning fiery furnace, and he will deliver us
> out of your hand, O king. But if not, be it known
> to you, O king, that we will not serve your gods
> or worship the golden image that you have set
> up." (3:16–18)

In chapter 4, God spoke through signs and wonders to Nebuchadnezzar. God gave revelation directly to this pagan king, and he not only acknowledged what he received was from God, but he announced it to the subjects of his kingdom!

> It has seemed good to me to show the signs and
> wonders that the Most High God has done for
> me. How great are his signs, how mighty his
> wonders! His kingdom is an everlasting king-
> dom, and his dominion endures from generation
> to generation. (4:2–3)

In spite of his amazing affirmation of the Most High God, the king had a dream that frightened him. "I saw a dream that made me afraid. As I lay in bed the fancies and the visions of my head alarmed me" (4:5). Nebuchadnezzar articulated the dream in verses 13–18. The meaning of the dream and Daniel's counsel from God to Nebuchadnezzar was recorded.

> This is the interpretation, O king: It is a decree of the Most High, which has come upon my lord the king, that you shall be driven from among men, and your dwelling shall be with the beasts of the field. You shall be made to eat grass like an ox, and you shall be wet with the dew of heaven, and seven periods of time shall pass over you, till you know that the Most High rules the kingdom of men and gives it to whom he will. And as it was commanded to leave the stump of the roots of the tree, your kingdom shall be confirmed for you from the time that you know that Heaven rules. Therefore, O king, let my counsel be acceptable to you: break off your sins by practicing righteousness, and your iniquities by showing mercy to the oppressed, that there may perhaps be a lengthening of your prosperity. (4:24–27)

An audible voice from heaven came directly to Nebuchadnezzar. This was not from Daniel, who was relaying a message; this was from the Lord, directly to the king.

> While the words were still in the king's mouth, there fell a voice from heaven, "O King Nebuchadnezzar, to you it is spoken: The kingdom has departed from you, and you shall be driven from among men, and your dwelling shall be with the beasts of the field. And you shall be made to eat grass like an ox, and seven periods of

time shall pass over you, until you know that the
Most High rules the kingdom of men and gives
it to whom he will." (4:31–32)

Daniel recorded another method of God's revelation in chapter
5 with handwriting on the wall, which announced the destruction of
Babylon.

Immediately the fingers of a human hand appeared
and wrote on the plaster of the wall of the king's
palace, opposite the lampstand. And the king
saw the hand as it wrote. Then the king's color
changed, and his thoughts alarmed him; his limbs
gave way, and his knees knocked together. (5:5–6)

This may be the most unusual form of revelation from God
that we have witnessed! Daniel gave the interpretation, explaining
the reason for the judgment.

And you his son, Belshazzar, have not humbled your heart, though you knew all this, but
you have lifted up yourself against the Lord of
heaven… This is the interpretation of the matter:
MENE, God has numbered the days of your kingdom and brought it to an end; TEKEL, you have
been weighed in the balances and found wanting;
PERES, your kingdom is divided and given to the
Medes and Persians. (5:22–28)

The interpretation of the writing and the fulfillment of that
interpretation occurred that very night.

Daniel not only was called upon to interpret the dreams of
others, he was also personally given dreams and visions from God
to record and interpret. In chapter 7 of the prophecy, Daniel had a
vision of four beasts (7:1–14). He "wrote down the dream." "I saw in
my vision" (v. 2). The interpretation was given in 7:15 ff. According

to verse 16, it appears that the vision was interactive. "I approached one of those who stood there." This may have been an angel. In verse 23, "Thus he said" apparently was the same one Daniel had approached in verse 16.

In chapter 8, Daniel recorded a vision of a ram and a goat (8:1–14). The first vision was in the first year of Belshazzar (chapter 7). This vision came in the third year of Belshazzar. Daniel's prophecy is obviously not chronological. During the vision, Daniel explained,

> Then I heard a holy one speaking, and another holy one said to the one who spoke, "For how long is the vision concerning the regular burnt offering, the transgression that makes desolate, and the giving over of the sanctuary and host to be trampled underfoot?" And he said to me, "For 2,300 evenings and mornings. Then the sanctuary shall be restored to its rightful state." (8:13–14)

The interpretation was recorded in 8:15 ff. We are specifically told that the angel Gabriel gave the interpretation to Daniel, apparently "face-to-face."

> And I heard a man's voice between the banks of the Ulai, and it called, "Gabriel, make this man understand the vision." So he came near where I stood. And when he came, I was frightened and fell on my face. But he said to me, "Understand, O son of man, that the vision is for the time of the end." (8:16–17).

The final instructions had a profound effect on Daniel.

> "The vision of the evenings and the mornings that has been told is true, but seal up the vision, for it refers to many days from now." And I, Daniel,

was overcome and lay sick for some days. Then I
rose and went about the king's business, but I was
appalled by the vision and did not understand it.
(8:26–27)

Daniel again received revelation from the angel Gabriel
recorded in chapter 9. We should not overlook verse 2, where Daniel
was studying the prophecy of Jeremiah, understanding the length of
Judah's captivity to be seventy years. It was as he was considering the
Scripture and praying that he received further revelation.

While I was speaking in prayer, the man Gabriel,
whom I had seen in the vision at the first, came
to me in swift flight at the time of the evening
sacrifice. He made me understand, speaking with
me and saying, "O Daniel, I have now come out
to give you insight and understanding. At the
beginning of your pleas for mercy a word went
out, and I have come to tell it to you, for you are
greatly loved. Therefore, consider the word and
understand the vision." (9:21–23)

The vision was explained by Gabriel in 9:24–27.

In 10:1, Daniel received yet another vision. We are told that
Daniel "understood the word and had understanding of the vision,"
suggesting that there were times when the prophets of God received
revelation that they did not understand. There was an interesting
exchange between Daniel and a messenger from God, who may have
been an angel or a pre-incarnate appearance of Jesus. Though there
were others present with Daniel, he alone saw the vision. The others were afraid and ran away to hide. God's love and approval was
acknowledged (v. 11). The messenger spoke of a confrontation with
the "prince of the kingdom of Persia" (v. 13), presumably an unholy
angel who had withstood the messenger for twenty-one days but was
helped by Michael, "one of the chief princes." The vision was "for
days yet to come." Perhaps it was a second messenger, described as

"one in the likeness of the children of man," that touched Daniel's lips (v. 16), allowing him to speak. Perhaps that same messenger or yet another one touched Daniel and strengthened the exhausted and emotionally drained prophet and told him what was to come. Chapter 11:1 through 12:3 outlines the prophecy the messenger shared with Daniel.

Daniel's prophecy ended with the announcement of a time of trouble greater than any the people of God had ever experienced, but after that, many would be delivered, which would include those "whose name shall be found written in the book." Daniel was instructed to "shut up the words and seal the book until the time of the end." That instruction was followed by further revelation involving "two others" (12:5) and someone else speaking to them, asking, "How long shall it be till the end of these wonders?" As Daniel listened to the exchange, he asked about the outcome of these things (v. 8) and was told,

> Go your way, Daniel, for the words are shut up
> and sealed until the time of the end. (v. 9)

> But go your way till the end. And you shall rest
> and shall stand in your allotted place at the end
> of the days. (v. 13)

The prophet Jeremiah was an early contemporary of Daniel, writing prior to and during the Babylonian captivity. We are immediately made aware that the words of Jeremiah are mostly the words of God that were given to him as God spoke His revelation.

> The word of Jeremiah...to whom the word of the
> Lord came. (vv. 1–2)

> The word of the Lord came to me saying. (v. 4)

> But the Lord said to me. (vv. 7–8)

> Then the Lord put out his hand and touched my
> mouth. And the Lord said to me. (v. 9)

As we have seen in some of the other prophetic books, most of the content in Jeremiah's writing is the Lord speaking. This can be seen throughout the remainder of chapter 1 (vv. 11–19) continuing through chapters 2–4 (2:1, 5, 31; 3:1, 6, 11, 14, 16, 19, 20; 4:1, 3, etc.) There were direct prophecies to the "faithless people" and the "men of Judah."

> Therefore thus says the LORD, the God of hosts:
> "Because you have spoken this word, behold, I
> am making my words in your mouth a fire, and
> this people wood, and the fire shall consume
> them." (5:14)

Jeremiah seemed to struggle with some of the content that the Lord was revealing to him to be delivered to the people.

> Then I said, "Ah, Lord GOD, surely you have
> utterly deceived this people and Jerusalem, say-
> ing, 'It shall be well with you,' whereas the sword
> has reached their very life." (4:10; also see 12:1 ff.)

There were times when the revelation God gave His prophet included a command for Jeremiah to be involved as an object lesson to the people (See 13:1 ff., a linen loincloth; 19:1 ff., a potter's earthenware flask; and 24:1 ff., figs). Jeremiah was commanded to go certain places where God would give him His message (18:1 ff., the potter's house). He was told to deliver difficult messages such as the strong words against lying prophets.

> I have heard what the prophets have said who
> prophesy lies in my name, saying, "I have
> dreamed, I have dreamed!" How long shall there
> be lies in the heart of the prophets who proph-

esy lies, and who prophesy the deceit of their own heart, who think to make my people forget my name by their dreams that they tell one another, even as their fathers forgot my name for Baal? Let the prophet who has a dream tell the dream but let him who has my word speak my word faithfully. What has straw in common with wheat? declares the LORD. Is not my word like fire, declares the LORD, and like a hammer that breaks the rock in pieces? Therefore, behold, I am against the prophets, declares the LORD, who steal my words from one another. Behold, I am against the prophets, declares the LORD, who use their tongues and declare, "declares the LORD." Behold, I am against those who prophesy lying dreams, declares the LORD, and who tell them and lead my people astray by their lies and their recklessness, when I did not send them or charge them. So, they do not profit this people at all, declares the LORD. (23:25–32)

It was, at times, very difficult to distinguish between true and false prophets as demonstrated in the exchange between Hananiah and Jeremiah in chapter 28.

In that same year…Hananiah the son of Azzur, the prophet from Gibeon, spoke to me in the house of the LORD, in the presence of the priests and all the people, saying, "Thus says the LORD of hosts, the God of Israel: I have broken the yoke of the king of Babylon. Within two years I will bring back to this place all the vessels of the LORD's house, which Nebuchadnezzar king of Babylon took away from this place and carried to Babylon. I will also bring back to this place Jeconiah the son of Jehoiakim, king of Judah, and

all the exiles from Judah who went to Babylon,
declares the LORD, for I will break the yoke of
the king of Babylon." Then the prophet Jeremiah
spoke to Hananiah the prophet in the presence
of the priests and all the people who were standing in the house of the LORD, and the prophet
Jeremiah said, "Amen! May the LORD do so; may
the LORD make the words that you have prophesied come true and bring back to this place from
Babylon the vessels of the house of the LORD,
and all the exiles. Yet hear now this word that I
speak in your hearing and in the hearing of all the
people. The prophets who preceded you and me
from ancient times prophesied war, famine, and
pestilence against many countries and great kingdoms. As for the prophet who prophesies peace,
when the word of that prophet comes to pass,
then it will be known that the LORD has truly
sent the prophet." Then the prophet Hananiah
took the yoke-bars from the neck of Jeremiah the
prophet and broke them. And Hananiah spoke
in the presence of all the people, saying, "Thus
says the LORD: Even so will I break the yoke of
Nebuchadnezzar king of Babylon from the neck
of all the nations within two years." But Jeremiah
the prophet went his way. Sometime after the
prophet Hananiah had broken the yoke-bars from
off the neck of Jeremiah the prophet, the word of
the LORD came to Jeremiah: "Go, tell Hananiah,
'Thus says the LORD: You have broken wooden
bars, but you have made in their place bars of
iron. For thus says the LORD of hosts, the God
of Israel: I have put upon the neck of all these
nations an iron yoke to serve Nebuchadnezzar
king of Babylon, and they shall serve him, for I
have given to him even the beasts of the field.'"

> And Jeremiah the prophet said to the prophet
> Hananiah, "Listen, Hananiah, the LORD has not
> sent you, and you have made this people trust
> in a lie. Therefore thus says the LORD: 'Behold,
> I will remove you from the face of the earth.
> This year you shall die, because you have uttered
> rebellion against the LORD.'" In that same year, in
> the seventh month, the prophet Hananiah died.

Throughout the prophecy, Jeremiah was given instruction to announce the revelations against Judah (4:5). An example of one of those messages occurs in chapters 7–10. God would speak to Jeremiah, and Jeremiah would relay that message to the people.

> For twenty-three years, from the thirteenth year
> of Josiah the son of Amon, king of Judah, to this
> day, the word of the LORD has come to me, and I
> have spoken persistently to you, but you have not
> listened. You have neither listened nor inclined
> your ears to hear, although the LORD persistently
> sent to you all his servants the prophets, saying,
> "Turn now, every one of you, from his evil way
> and evil deeds, and dwell upon the land that the
> LORD has given to you and your fathers from of
> old and forever. Do not go after other gods to
> serve and worship them or provoke me to anger
> with the work of your hands. Then I will do
> you no harm." Yet you have not listened to me,
> declares the LORD, that you might provoke me to
> anger with the work of your hands to your own
> harm. (25:3–7)

As we have seen throughout this study, what the prophets said was considered to be what God was saying.

Some of the prophecies were personal (20:1 ff.; 22:18 ff.; 29:1 ff.; 45:2 ff.). There were times when a prophecy was requested by the leaders of Judah.

> Inquire of the LORD for us, for Nebuchadnezzar king of Babylon is making war against us. Perhaps the LORD will deal with us according to all his wonderful deeds and will make him withdraw from us. (21:2 ff.)

Often prophesying against Judah and the false prophets got Jeremiah in serious trouble. Jeremiah was told, "do not hold back a word" (26:1), and he didn't, but the people "laid hold of him saying, 'You shall die'" (26:8).

Jeremiah was instructed at times to write down in a book the words that the Lord had spoken. No doubt, at least part of what he recorded is contained in the book we have today.

> Thus says the Lord, the God of Israel: Write in a book all the words that I have spoken to you. (30:2)
> Take a scroll and write on it all the words that I have spoken to you against Israel and Judah and all the nations. (36:2)

Jeremiah dictated to his amanuensis, Baruch, and instructed him to go to the temple and read the words that were recorded. Eventually the scroll was given to the king, who cut it apart and burned it with fire. However, the Lord came to Jeremiah again and instructed him to dictate a second time to Baruch the former words that had been written on the destroyed scroll. God also had a message to add for the king who burned the first scroll. At the end of Jeremiah's prophecy,

> The word that Jeremiah the prophet commanded Seraiah the son of Neriah, son of Mahseiah, when he went with Zedekiah king of Judah to Babylon,

in the fourth year of his reign. Seraiah was the quartermaster. Jeremiah wrote in a book all the disaster that should come upon Babylon, all these words that are written concerning Babylon. And Jeremiah said to Seraiah: "When you come to Babylon, see that you read all these words, and say, 'O LORD, you have said concerning this place that you will cut it off, so that nothing shall dwell in it, neither man nor beast, and it shall be desolate forever.' When you finish reading this book, tie a stone to it and cast it into the midst of the Euphrates, and say, 'Thus shall Babylon sink, to rise no more, because of the disaster that I am bringing upon her, and they shall become exhausted.'" Thus far are the words of Jeremiah. (51:59–64)

A contemporary of Jeremiah was Habakkuk. This prophet prophesied at the beginning of the Babylonian captivity. His frustration was with God. How could (or why would) God allow an empire whose evil exceeded Judah's sin to judge Judah? "If God is in control, why does evil so often win?" Habakkuk asked the question, and God answered! The revelation from the Lord came quickly to the prophet, "Look among the nations and see, wonder and be astounded" (1:5). God was about to raise up the Chaldeans (the Babylonians) to bring judgment upon Judah.

Habakkuk continued to struggle to understand how God could use the wicked to bring judgment on His own people!

You who are of purer eyes than to see evil and cannot look at wrong, why do you idly look at traitors and remain silent when the wicked swallows up the man more righteous than he? (1:13)

In chapter 2, the Lord answered, calling upon Habakkuk to write down the vision of the judgments that would come upon the

Chaldeans. The final chapter was a prayer of Habakkuk to the Lord acknowledging the Lord's word to him. Habakkuk's prayer ended in rejoicing. There is no clear statement as to the form of these revelations from God, but they appear to be a conversation that the Lord and Habakkuk had together. It is possible that the conversation was audible.

The words recorded by the prophet Zephaniah were written a few years before Habakkuk, somewhere between 640 and 612 BC. Zephaniah's prophecy was written to Judah, warning the nation of impending judgment, but also reminding the nation of God's mercy. The revelation opens with, "The word of the Lord that came to Zephaniah" (1:1). Unlike the prophecy of Habakkuk, there is no conversation or interaction between God and the prophet. The entire prophecy from the first verse to the last is God speaking.

The prophecy of Ezekiel occurred about the same time as Daniel, Jeremiah, and Habakkuk. The first group of Israelites were deported to Babylon about 605 BC. The prophet Daniel was in this group. A second group of Jews was deported about 597 BC, which included Ezekiel, who was probably about twenty-five years old at the time. Ezekiel was taken to Tel-abib near the canal Chebar (3:15). Here he lived in his own house with his beloved wife (8:1; 24:16 ff.). Five years after Ezekiel came to Tel-abib, he was called to be a prophet of God (592 BC). That was about six years before the destruction of Jerusalem. While Jeremiah was ministering to the people back home, Ezekiel was preaching to the Jews who were in captivity in Babylon. Chapters 1–24 were all given before the siege of Jerusalem, chapters 25–32 during the siege, and chapters 33–48 after the siege. Though the prophet was in distant Babylonia, he was able to see events in Jerusalem through the power of the Spirit of God.

The prophecy opened with Ezekiel declaring that "the heavens were opened, and I saw visions of God" (1:1). In verse 3, "the hand of the Lord was upon him there." This vision continues through 3:27. The vision was of the glory of God.

> Like the appearance of the bow that is in the
> cloud on the day of rain, so was the appearance of

the brightness all around. Such was the appearance of the likeness of the glory of the LORD. And when I saw it, I fell on my face, and I heard the voice of one speaking. (1:28)

While experiencing the vision, the Lord spoke.

And he said to me, "Son of man, stand on your feet, and I will speak with you." And as he spoke to me, the Spirit entered into me and set me on my feet, and I heard him speaking to me. (2:1–2)

In chapter 3, Ezekiel recorded,

Then the Spirit lifted me up, and I heard behind me the voice of a great earthquake: "Blessed be the glory of the LORD from its place!"... The Spirit lifted me up and took me away, and I went in bitterness in the heat of my spirit, the hand of the LORD being strong upon me... And the hand of the LORD was upon me there. And he said to me, "Arise, go out into the valley, and there I will speak with you." So I arose and went out into the valley, and behold, the glory of the LORD stood there, like the glory that I had seen by the Chebar canal, and I fell on my face. But the Spirit entered into me and set me on my feet, and he spoke with me and said to me, "Go, shut yourself within your house. And you, O son of man, behold, cords will be placed upon you, and you shall be bound with them, so that you cannot go out among the people. And I will make your tongue cling to the roof of your mouth, so that you shall be mute and unable to reprove them, for they are a rebellious house. But when I speak with you, I will open your mouth, and you shall

> say to them, 'Thus says the Lord GOD.' He who
> will hear, let him hear; and he who will refuse
> to hear, let him refuse, for they are a rebellious
> house." (3:22–27)

Throughout the entire prophecy, we will see, "The word of the Lord came to me."

Ezekiel was told to take various things: a brick in 4:1; and wheat, barley, etc. in 4:9. In chapter 5 Ezekiel was instructed to take a sharp sword (5:1) to cut off his hair and to weigh it and divide it. In chapter 6, Ezekiel was told to face the mountains and prophesy against them (6:1). In chapter 8, the prophet was instructed to dig into and through a wall in the temple to view the abominations going on within. In chapter 10, Ezekiel was to fill his hands with burning coals.

> In the sixth year, in the sixth month, on the fifth
> day of the month, as I sat in my house, with the
> elders of Judah sitting before me, the hand of the
> Lord GOD fell upon me there. Then I looked, and
> behold, a form that had the appearance of a man.
> Below what appeared to be his waist was fire, and
> above his waist was something like the appear-
> ance of brightness, like gleaming metal. He put
> out the form of a hand and took me by a lock
> of my head, and the Spirit lifted me up between
> earth and heaven and brought me in visions of
> God to Jerusalem, to the entrance of the gateway
> of the inner court that faces north, where was
> the seat of the image of jealousy, which provokes
> to jealousy. And behold, the glory of the God of
> Israel was there, like the vision that I saw in the
> valley. (8:1–4)

This one who had the appearance as a man continued to speak. "He cried in my ears with a loud voice" (9:1).

Beginning in 9:7, there was the dramatic and symbolic vision of the departure of the glory of the Lord from the city of Jerusalem.

> Then the glory of the LORD went out from the threshold of the house and stood over the cherubim. And the cherubim lifted up their wings and mounted up from the earth before my eyes as they went out, with the wheels beside them. And they stood at the entrance of the east gate of the house of the LORD, and the glory of the God of Israel was over them. (10:18–19)

Chapter 11 records the completion of the vision of the departure of the glory of God from Israel.

> Then the cherubim lifted up their wings, with the wheels beside them, and the glory of the God of Israel was over them. And the glory of the LORD went up from the midst of the city and stood on the mountain that is on the east side of the city. And the Spirit lifted me up and brought me in the vision by the Spirit of God into Chaldea, to the exiles. Then the vision that I had seen went up from me. And I told the exiles all the things that the LORD had shown me. (11:22–25)

Similar to Jeremiah's prophecy, Ezekiel was instructed by the Lord to prophesy against the false prophets:

> The word of the LORD came to me: "Son of man, prophesy against the prophets of Israel, who are prophesying, and say to those who prophesy from their own hearts: 'Hear the word of the LORD!' Thus says the Lord GOD, Woe to the foolish prophets who follow their own spirit and have seen nothing! Your prophets have been like

jackals among ruins, O Israel. You have not gone up into the breaches or built up a wall for the house of Israel, that it might stand in battle in the day of the LORD. They have seen false visions and lying divinations. They say, 'Declares the LORD,' when the LORD has not sent them, and yet they expect him to fulfill their word. Have you not seen a false vision and uttered a lying divination, whenever you have said, 'Declares the LORD,' although I have not spoken?" (13:1–7)

The judgment against them was scathing (13:19–23)!

Judgment was coming, and there was no turning it away. With surprising words, the Lord came to Ezekiel:

Son of man, when a land sins against me by acting faithlessly, and I stretch out my hand against it and break its supply of bread and send famine upon it, and cut off from it man and beast, even if these three men, Noah, Daniel, and Job, were in it, they would deliver but their own lives by their righteousness, declares the Lord GOD. (14:13–14)

Though this affirms the righteousness and significance of Noah and Daniel and Job, it also establishes the immutable purposes of God. What God had determined would not be altered. Israel would be destroyed and carried away into captivity. In fact, the Lord instructed Ezekiel to "write down the name of this day, this very day. The king of Babylon has laid siege to Jerusalem this very day" (24:2).

The Lord made the case to and through Ezekiel regarding His holy name.

Therefore say to the house of Israel, Thus says the Lord GOD: It is not for your sake, O house of Israel, that I am about to act, but for the sake of

my holy name, which you have profaned among
the nations to which you came. And I will vindicate the holiness of my great name, which has
been profaned among the nations, and which
you have profaned among them. And the nations
will know that I am the LORD, declares the Lord
GOD, when through you I vindicate my holiness before their eyes. I will take you from the
nations and gather you from all the countries
and bring you into your own land. I will sprinkle
clean water on you, and you shall be clean from
all your uncleannesses, and from all your idols I
will cleanse you. And I will give you a new heart,
and a new spirit I will put within you. And I will
remove the heart of stone from your flesh and
give you a heart of flesh. And I will put my Spirit
within you and cause you to walk in my statutes
and be careful to obey my rules. You shall dwell
in the land that I gave to your fathers, and you
shall be my people, and I will be your God. And I
will deliver you from all your uncleannesses. And
I will summon the grain and make it abundant
and lay no famine upon you. I will make the fruit
of the tree and the increase of the field abundant,
that you may never again suffer the disgrace of
famine among the nations. Then you will remember your evil ways, and your deeds that were not
good, and you will loathe yourselves for your
iniquities and your abominations. It is not for
your sake that I will act, declares the Lord GOD;
let that be known to you. Be ashamed and con-
founded for your ways, O house of Israel. Thus
says the Lord GOD: On the day that I cleanse
you from all your iniquities, I will cause the cities to be inhabited, and the waste places shall be
rebuilt. And the land that was desolate shall be

tilled, instead of being the desolation that it was
in the sight of all who passed by. And they will
say, "This land that was desolate has become like
the garden of Eden, and the waste and desolate
and ruined cities are now fortified and inhabited." Then the nations that are left all around
you shall know that I am the Lord; I have rebuilt
the ruined places and replanted that which was
desolate. I am the Lord; I have spoken, and I will
do it. Thus says the Lord God: This also I will
let the house of Israel ask me to do for them: to
increase their people like a flock. Like the flock
for sacrifices, like the flock at Jerusalem during
her appointed feasts, so shall the waste cities be
filled with flocks of people. Then they will know
that I am the Lord. (36:22–38)

The prophecy of Ezekiel concludes as the prophet received a
vision of a new temple and a new day (chapters 40–48). The glory
that had departed would return.

As the glory of the Lord entered the temple by
the gate facing east, the Spirit lifted me up and
brought me into the inner court; and behold, the
glory of the Lord filled the temple. (43:4–5)

Haggai's prophecy was written after the Babylonian captivity
(around 520 BC). In 538, Cyrus, the king of Persia, had allowed
many to return to Judah. Though the temple project had been started
some sixteen years earlier, construction had ceased. This prophecy was
directed to Zerubbabel, the governor, and to Joshua, the high priest.
"The Word of the Lord came by the hand of Haggai the prophet to
Zerubbabel" (1:1). That same phrase is repeated in verse 3. "Thus
says the Lord of hosts" (1:2). Haggai spoke as the mouthpiece for the
Lord, "Then Haggai, the messenger of the Lord, spoke to the people
with the Lord's message, 'I am with you, declares the Lord'" (1:13).

In chapter 2, the word of the Lord came to the prophet twice on the same day. The first time the message was for the priests, and the second time the message was personal, for Zerubbabel:

> The word of the LORD came a second time to Haggai on the twenty-fourth day of the month, "Speak to Zerubbabel, governor of Judah, saying, I am about to shake the heavens and the earth, and to overthrow the throne of kingdoms. I am about to destroy the strength of the kingdoms of the nations and overthrow the chariots and their riders. And the horses and their riders shall go down, every one by the sword of his brother. On that day, declares the LORD of hosts, I will take you, O Zerubbabel my servant, the son of Shealtiel, declares the LORD, and make you like a signet ring, for I have chosen you, declares the LORD of hosts." (2:20–23)

The prophet Zechariah was written about the same time as Haggai. Through Zechariah, God gave the nation a vision of His purposes beyond the restored temple. "The word of the Lord came to the prophet Zechariah" (1:1; 4:8; 6:9; 7:1; 7:4; 7:8; 8:1; 8:18; 11:4; 11:15). The words from the Lord were to be spoken as from the Lord to the people:

> The LORD was very angry with your fathers. Therefore say to them, Thus declares the LORD of hosts: Return to me, says the LORD of hosts, and I will return to you, says the LORD of hosts. Do not be like your fathers, to whom the former prophets cried out, "Thus says the LORD of hosts, Return from your evil ways and from your evil deeds." But they did not hear or pay attention to me, declares the LORD. Your fathers, where are they? And the prophets, do they live forever? But

my words and my statutes, which I commanded
my servants the prophets, did they not overtake
your fathers? So they repented and said, "As the
LORD of hosts purposed to deal with us for our
ways and deeds, so has he dealt with us." (1:2–6)

Zechariah was given numerous visions. In chapter 1, a night
vision came from an angel (1:8 ff.) who acted as the spokesperson,
telling Zechariah what the Lord was saying (1:14–17). The Lord was
showing Zechariah various things, and the angel was explaining what
the prophet was seeing (1:18–20). Other visions were recorded in the
first six chapters of the book. There were also numerous messianic
prophecies contained in this book (3:8–9; 9:9 ff.; 12:10 ff.; 14:3 ff.).

The final prophecy in the OT is Malachi. It was presented as an
oracle from God given to the prophet. Similar to what we have seen
in the other prophets, Malachi was essentially a prophecy from God
to the people. It came through Malachi, but there is no interaction
recorded between the prophet and God. The prophecy concerning
the messenger to prepare the way for the Lord (chapters 3 and 4)
would surface in the NT in regard to the ministry of John the Baptist
as he prepared the way for the coming of Messiah, the Lord Jesus.

Before we leave the OT, we need to consider Ezra and Nehemiah,
two canonical books that were written as the Babylonian captivity
was coming to an end. Ezra and Nehemiah are more historical nar-
ratives than the prophets and prophecies we have examined. The
accounts of God speaking are more like what we saw in the historical
books of Samuel and the Kings and Chronicles than in the prophets.
However, we still see the revelation of God. These books are considered here chronologically at the end of the OT era.

Ezra opens with reference to the prophet Jeremiah and what
he wrote, which was described as the Word of the Lord spoken by
Jeremiah. It was a pagan king who acted to fulfill the Word of the
Lord with this impressive proclamation:

Thus says Cyrus king of Persia: The LORD, the
God of heaven, has given me all the kingdoms of

the earth, and he has charged me to build him a house at Jerusalem, which is in Judah. Whoever is among you of all his people, may his God be with him, and let him go up to Jerusalem, which is in Judah, and rebuild the house of the LORD, the God of Israel—he is the God who is in Jerusalem. And let each survivor, in whatever place he sojourns, be assisted by the men of his place with silver and gold, with goods and with beasts, besides freewill offerings for the house of God that is in Jerusalem. (1:2–4)

Contained in this historical narrative were affirmations of the OT as the Word of God. As Zerubbabel and others were reconstructing the altar of God on which to sacrifice burnt offerings, they followed what Moses had recorded in the Law (3:2 ff.). As work began on rebuilding the house of God, Ezra referenced the ministries of the prophets Haggai and Zechariah (5:1 ff.) who were carrying out their prophetic ministries at that time. Throughout the book, it is clear that the author loved the Law of God and treated it as the very Word of God. "For Ezra had set his heart to study the Law of the LORD, and to do it and to teach his statutes and rules in Israel" (7:10).

Nehemiah was a cupbearer for the king of Persia. He was aware of the rebuilding efforts in Jerusalem in regard to the temple, but word came to him concerning the condition of the city and the broken-down walls that once surrounded it. Distraught, Nehemiah began to pray. Like Ezra, Nehemiah was referencing the Word of God:

We have acted very corruptly against you and have not kept the commandments, the statutes, and the rules that you commanded your servant Moses. Remember the word that you commanded your servant Moses, saying, "If you are unfaithful, I will scatter you among the peoples, but if you return to me and keep my commandments and do them, though your outcasts are in

129

the uttermost parts of heaven, from there I will
gather them and bring them to the place that
I have chosen, to make my name dwell there."
(1:7–10)

Later, after the completion of the wall around the city, Nehemiah
was involved in various reforms. The people were gathered as Ezra,
the scribe, opened the book of the Law of Moses and began to read.
The response of the people is instructive: "For all the people wept as
they heard the words of the Law" (8:9). Following the weeping and
the repenting, there was great rejoicing and worship and commit-
ment in the form of making a firm covenant with the Lord. There are
no references referring to God speaking to Ezra or Nehemiah apart
from the written Word in the Law of Moses. That is a significant
departure from what we have seen.

With that, we conclude our observations of the history of God
speaking in the Old Testament. What have we seen? Wayne Grudem,
in his book, *The Gift of Prophecy*, made the case that there are no
incidents in the OT where the hearers evaluated or sifted through
the words of the prophets, sorting out the good words from the bad,
the true words from the false.[8] For example, in 1 Samuel 3:19, "And
Samuel grew, and the Lord was with him and let none of his words
fall to the ground." As a prophet of God, it was said of Samuel,
"Behold, there is a man of God in this city, and he is a man who is
held in honor, all that he says comes true" (1 Sam. 9:6). As we have
learned, when a prophet spoke in the name of the Lord, if any of
those prophecies did not come true, this one was declared to be a
false prophet. He didn't just miss that particular prophecy, but perhaps he'll get the next one correct; he was a false prophet! And the
authority attached to prophets was so great that to prophesy falsely
meant death to that prophet. In other words, the prophet was judged
to be true or false, not just the words he was saying. To disobey the
words of a true prophet was to disobey God.

---

8. Wayne A. Grudem, *The Gift of Prophecy in the New Testament
Today* (Wheaton, IL: Crossway Books, 1988), 20–23.

It seems that all of the OT was thought to have been written by those who at least functioned as prophets by the authority of God—that even the very words they spoke (and wrote) were from God Himself. Luke records Jesus's words to the Emmaus couple after His resurrection:

> And he said to them, "O foolish ones, and slow of heart to believe all that the prophets have spoken! Was it not necessary that the Christ should suffer these things and enter into his glory?" And beginning with Moses and all the Prophets, he interpreted to them in all the Scriptures the things concerning himself. (Luke 24:25–27)

Luke's words are instructive. "*All that the prophets* have spoken…beginning with Moses and *all the Prophets*, he interpreted to them in *all the Scriptures* the things concerning himself." The sense seems to be that all of the OT text was considered as having been given by God through the prophets.

As we have seen, the prophets received the word from the Lord in various ways (visions, dreams, voices, angels and the angel of the Lord, a burning bush, writing on the wall, etc.), but what they received was from the Lord. And God spoke through them, not randomly to various people of Israel or other nations giving personal directives or promises or insights or messages or promptings. The words came through the prophets. This is exactly what the author of Hebrews was saying in Hebrews 1:1–2:

> Long ago, at many times and in many ways, God spoke to our fathers by the prophets, but in these last days he has spoken to us by his Son, whom he appointed the heir of all things, through whom also he created the world.

The task before us now is to see how God has spoken by His Son.

8

God Speaks through His Son—the Gospels

As we move on to the New Testament to discover how God spoke through His Son, we need to remember that there were four hundred years of silence between the testaments. It is interesting that before the OT was recorded, starting with Moses and the Law, there was a four-hundred-year "silence" while the people were in bondage in Egypt. We have literally observed how "In the past God spoke to our forefathers through the prophets at many times and in various ways." We are now about to come face-to-face with the remainder of that verse, "but in these last days he has spoken to us by His Son."

Not since the fall of man in the garden of Eden had man and God walked together. In the garden, Adam was in the state of untested holiness until he chose to disobey God's direct command and was then rejected by God and cast out of the garden. As we have seen, there were occasions when God interacted with various people in the OT, but nothing like what we are about to witness in the NT. People remained separated from God because of sin, but God came in flesh to actually dwell among humanity and communicate face-to-face with them. The second person of the triune God was veiled in human flesh, in some sense "laying aside" the use of some of His attributes, though retaining His absolute deity, and He dwelt among us!

All that Jesus said in the Gospels is a record of God speaking. All that the Gospel writers wrote as commentary on what Jesus said is also God speaking. The entire NT was "carried along" by the Holy Spirit as Peter expressed in 2 Peter 1:20–21. The Gospel accounts were no longer visions or dreams or words from God through prophets. They were the actual words of God spoken by God incarnate, speaking face-to-face with sinful people!

We start our consideration of the NT with a brief look at the prologue in the Gospel according to John. There are many ways to communicate. We could show pictures, or we could make signs to call attention to what we want to make known. Or we can use words. Words are expressive. While it has been said that one picture is worth a thousand words, we can do with words what we cannot do with pictures. We can express things that we cannot see or show or illustrate any other way. We can speak words, or we can record words on paper or text words on our phones. God chose to make Himself known through words, and His greatest revelation of Himself came to us through His Son, and God chose to call Him "the Word." The Word is the expression of God and the revelation of God.

The first words that would speak of the Son would come through angels. These heavenly messengers would announce the coming births of the prophesied forerunner of Jesus, John, as well as the Son of God Himself. Luke recorded God's revelation to Zechariah concerning the birth of John the Baptist. Is it any wonder Zechariah responded as he did since God had been silent for four hundred years? An angel of the Lord appeared to Zechariah (Luke 1:11) and spoke (1:13). Zechariah asked for some clarification, "How shall I know this?" (v. 18), knowing that he and his wife were old, and she had been barren throughout their marriage. From the angel Gabriel's answer (v. 19), we learn that Zechariah's response was one of unbelief (v. 20). Gabriel told Zechariah that he "was sent to speak to you and to bring you this good news" (v. 19). As Zechariah came out of the holy place of the temple, the people were convinced something supernatural had happened—"They realized he had seen a vision in the temple" (v. 22). That was surely prompted by Zechariah's inability to speak—a temporary judgment from God, due to his unbelief. The text may suggest more than a vision, perhaps an actual appearance of Gabriel to Zechariah. However, something similar happened to Joseph: "As he considered these things, behold an angel of the Lord appeared to him in a dream" (Matt. 1:20). We should understand, however, that a personal appearance, a dream, or a vision as recorded in the Scripture were each viewed the same—as God speaking! After John was born, Zechariah's voice returned, and Luke wrote that he was "filled with the Holy Spirit and prophesied."

The angel also had a message for Mary concerning John's birth as she was told about the pregnancy of her relative, Elizabeth (1:36). But the primary message to Mary was in regard to her having been chosen to give birth to the Lord Jesus. Luke writes,

> The angel Gabriel was sent from God to a city of Galilee named Nazareth to a virgin betrothed to a man whose name was Joseph, of the house of David. And the virgin's name was Mary... And the angel said to her, "Do not be afraid, Mary, for you have found favor with God. And behold, you will conceive in your womb and bear a son, and you shall call his name Jesus. He will be great and will be called the Son of the Most High. And the Lord God will give to him the throne of his father David, and he will reign over the house of Jacob forever, and of his kingdom there will be no end." And Mary said to the angel, "How will this be, since I am a virgin?" And the angel answered her, "The Holy Spirit will come upon you, and the power of the Most High will overshadow you; therefore the child to be born will be called holy—the Son of God." (Luke 1:26–27, 30–35)

An angel of the Lord, presumably Gabriel, also visited Joseph after he had become aware of Mary's pregnancy and "had resolved to divorce her quietly" (Matt. 1:19). The angel assured Joseph that the baby conceived was "from the Holy Spirit" (v. 20), confirming that Mary had not been unfaithful to her betrothal. Joseph was not to proceed as he had planned but was told to take Mary as his wife. This angelic prophecy included the name to be given to the baby. Matthew referenced the OT prophecy found in Isaiah 7:14 which predicted this event (v. 22).

An angel was also involved in the birth announcement that was given to the shepherds who were tending to their sheep on the hills outside of Bethlehem. This angel was joined by a multitude of heavenly hosts who gave glory to God concerning what had just occurred. This was not a dream or a vision but an event in real time and experience, witnessed by the shepherds (Luke 2:9 ff.).

After Jesus's birth, when it came time for the purification rites, Jesus was brought to the temple in Jerusalem. This was according to OT Law (Exod. 13:2, 12). While there, Mary and Joseph and Jesus encountered a man named Simeon. Luke records that the Holy Spirit had in some way revealed to him "that he would not see death before he had seen the Lord's Christ" (2:26). A prophecy about the child followed containing blessing for both Israel and the Gentiles (vv. 29–35).

Sometime after the purification of Mary and the meeting with Simeon, the family received a visit from magi from the East. There are multiple examples of God's revelation in regard to this visit. Details are sparse, but the magi saw an unusual luminary in the sky. They also seemed to know something about a prophecy concerning the King of the Jews. When they arrived in Jerusalem, they were asking questions concerning this one whom they believed had been born. It is quite possible they derived their information from the record of Daniel. Word of the visitors' mission got back to King Herod, and he summoned the chief priests and scribes to verify what the magi were saying. The scribes and chief priests were familiar enough with the OT revelation of God that they cited Micah's prophecy concerning the place where this King was to be born. Herod secretly summoned the magi to check on the timing of the birth and then sent them to find this king and to return to him with information regarding the child's whereabouts.

According to Matthew 2:12, the magi received a prophetic message in a dream, warning them not to return to Herod. When the magi departed, a prophecy came to Joseph in a dream, delivered by an angel (Matt. 2:13). Matthew connects this revelation with reference to the prophet Jeremiah concerning the slaughter of the babies in and around Bethlehem. There was a second dream, sometime later, making it known to Joseph that Herod had died, making it safe for Joseph and his family to return from Egypt (Matt. 2:19). This revelation came in the same form as the earlier warning.

God's revelation through His Son began when Jesus was about thirty. Matthew introduced the ministry of John with reference to the one who would "prepare the way of the Lord," as prophesied by Isaiah (Matt. 3:3; Luke 3:4 ff.; Mark 1:2). John's message was no doubt prophetic, but actual references concerning the speaking of God to John are not given, except for the quote from Isaiah's prophecy (Isa. 40:3). John, however, did prophesy concerning the identity of Lord Jesus following the time of the Lord's baptism.

> And John bore witness: "I saw the Spirit descend from heaven like a dove, and it remained on him. I myself did not know him, but he who sent me to baptize with water said to me, 'He on whom you see the Spirit descend and remain, this is he who baptizes with the Holy Spirit.' And I have seen and have borne witness that this is the Son of God." (John 1:29–34)

It is time to turn our attention to the words of Jesus as recorded by the Gospel writers. Actually, Jesus first recorded words were prior to His ministry, occurring at the temple when He was only twelve (Luke 2:41 ff.). Jesus had gone with His earthly parents from Nazareth to Jerusalem for the Feast of the Passover (Luke 2:41). As the traveling group left Jerusalem to return to their homes, Jesus was unintentionally left behind. When the frantic parents returned and found Him in the temple, He responded, "Why were you looking for me? Did you not know that I must be in my Father's house?" His first recorded words identified His relationship with the Heavenly Father.

As Jesus prepared to begin His ministry, He approached John and requested that He be baptized (Matt. 3:13 ff.; Mark 1:9–11). As Jesus came out of the water, praying (Luke 2:21), the Holy Spirit descended in a dove-like form, and a voice from the Father was heard: "This is my beloved Son in whom I am well pleased" (Matt.

3:17). Mark says that immediately after Jesus was baptized, that the Spirit "drove him out into the wilderness" (1:12). Jesus was in the wilderness forty days, being tempted by Satan (1:13). Matthew and Luke also included the temptations in their accounts (Matt. 4:1–11; Luke 4:1–13). There is no record of communication between Jesus and the Father during the temptation. There was, however, a conversation recorded between the Son of God and the devil (Matt. 4 and Luke 4). It is important to note that the Lord Jesus used the recorded Word of God (from Deuteronomy) to answer each of the temptations. It should also be noted that the devil also quoted scripture to Jesus (Ps. 91:11–12)! Following the devil's departure, the angels came and ministered to the Lord (Matt. 4:11).

There are several examples of conversation between Jesus and the religious leaders regarding Sabbath controversies. We consider two of those controversies. The first was when Jesus defended His disciples for eating grain on the Sabbath (Mark 2:23–28; Luke 6:1–5; Matt. 12:1–8).

> At that time Jesus went through the grain fields on the Sabbath. His disciples were hungry, and they began to pluck heads of grain and to eat. But when the Pharisees saw it, they said to him, "Look, your disciples are doing what is not lawful to do on the Sabbath." He said to them, "Have you not read what David did when he was hungry, and those who were with him: how he entered the house of God and ate the bread of the Presence, which it was not lawful for him to eat nor for those who were with him, but only for the priests? Or have you not read in the Law how on the Sabbath the priests in the temple profane the Sabbath and are guiltless? I tell you, something greater than the temple is here. And if you had known what this means, 'I desire mercy, and not sacrifice,' you would not have condemned

the guiltless. For the Son of Man is lord of the Sabbath."

According to OT revelation, what Jesus and His disciples did was not unlawful.

If you go into your neighbor's standing grain, you may pluck the ears with your hand, but you shall not put a sickle to your neighbor's standing grain. (Deut. 23:25)

Nevertheless, the Pharisees challenged the OT argument with their redefined and enhanced rabbinical tradition. To pick the grain and rub it in the hands to break loose the husks, and then to blow away the chaff and eat the grain, constituted the work of reaping and harvesting. Thus, according to rabbinic law, the disciples were guilty of work and thus guilty of breaking the Sabbath. According to the rabbis, there were thirty-nine kinds of work forbidden on the Sabbath. Jesus answered for His disciples, assuming responsibility for their action and justifying what they did. Jesus based His defense on five arguments. There was the argument from OT history, when He asked, "Have you not read...?" He followed that with the argument from the law. Clearly the priests worked on the Sabbath in the temple and were not charged with breaking Sabbath law. Next came the argument from the prophets. If the priests could work in the temple on the Sabbath and not break the Law, then One who was greater than the temple could "work" in this manner with His disciples and not violate Sabbath law. This was a claim to deity. The fourth argument was based on the original purpose of the Sabbath. "And he said to them, 'The Sabbath was made for man, not man for the Sabbath'" (Mark 2:27). God made man first, and then adapted the Sabbath for man. It was to be a day of rest, not toil. The final argument was a declaration of Jesus's superiority as being Lord of the Sabbath.

And the LORD said to Moses, "You are to speak to the people of Israel and say, 'Above all you shall keep my Sabbaths, for this is a sign between me and you throughout your generations, that you may know that I, the LORD, sanctify you.'" (Exod. 31:12–13)

The second Sabbath controversy to be considered was the healing of the man with the withered hand (Mark 3:1–6; Luke 6:6–11; Matt. 12:9–14).

He went on from there and entered their synagogue. And a man was there with a withered hand. And they asked him, "Is it lawful to heal on the Sabbath?"—so that they might accuse him. He said to them, "Which one of you who has a sheep, if it falls into a pit on the Sabbath, will not take hold of it and lift it out? Of how much more value is a man than a sheep! So it is lawful to do good on the Sabbath." Then he said to the man, "Stretch out your hand." And the man stretched it out, and it was restored, healthy like the other. But the Pharisees went out and conspired against him, how to destroy him. (Matt. 12:9–14)

Attempting to trap Jesus, the Pharisees assumed He would heal the man! Jesus reminded the religious leaders of their own Rabbinic law that they would not view the merciful deliverance of an animal that had fallen into a pit as breaking the Sabbath. If it was appropriate to do good on the Sabbath to help an animal, how would it be breaking the Law to help a human being? Mark wrote that Jesus looked around at the Pharisees "with anger, grieved at their hardness of heart," and then He healed the man! Jesus asked the man to do the very thing he could not do, and he did it! Jesus commanded the man, and he obeyed, and the power of Christ healed him.

As could be expected, the Pharisees did not marvel at Jesus's power, nor were they thankful that the man was now healed. Instead they exited the synagogue and conspired together against Jesus, considering how they might destroy Him. Mark tells us that they took counsel with the Herodians! There was no love between these two groups, but they now had a common enemy! Why did the Pharisees hate Jesus so much? There were many reasons. Among them was His claim to a unique relationship with God.

> The man went away and told the Jews that it was Jesus who had healed him. And this was why the Jews were persecuting Jesus, because he was doing these things on the Sabbath. But Jesus answered them, "My Father is working until now, and I am working." This was why the Jews were seeking all the more to kill him, because not only was he breaking the Sabbath, but he was even calling God his own Father, making himself equal with God. (John 5:15–18)

They hated Jesus because of His authoritative teaching. The scribes never claimed authority. They referred to Rabbi so-and-so, but such was not the case with Jesus. "You have heard…but I say unto you" (Matt. 5:21–22). Mark recorded,

> And they were astonished at his teaching, for he taught them as one who had authority, and not as the scribes. (Mark 1:22)

The Pharisees hated Jesus because of His power. They could not deny Jesus's power, but they claimed that it originated from a different source. They believed His power was coming from Satan. They also hated Jesus because of His association with tax collectors and sinners. Mark records,

> And the scribes of the Pharisees, when they saw that he was eating with sinners and tax collectors, said to his disciples, "Why does he eat with tax collectors and sinners?" (Mark 2:16)

Luke wrote,

> Now the tax collectors and sinners were all draw-
> ing near to hear him. And the Pharisees and the
> scribes grumbled, saying, "This man receives sin-
> ners and eats with them." (Luke 15:1–2)

They hated Him for that!
They also hated Jesus because of His attitude toward the Law.

> Do not think that I have come to abolish the Law
> or the Prophets; I have not come to abolish them
> but to fulfill them. (Matt. 5:17)

Finally, they hated Him for His claims. Consider, for example,
Jesus's claim with reference to His death and resurrection described
in terms of the temple being destroyed and then raised in three days.

> Jesus answered them, "Destroy this temple, and
> in three days I will raise it up." The Jews then
> said, "It has taken forty-six years to build this
> temple, and will you raise it up in three days?"
> (John 2:19–20).

> This man said, "I am able to destroy the temple
> of God, and to rebuild it in three days." (Matt.
> 26:61).

> We heard him say, "I will destroy this temple that
> is made with hands, and in three days I will build
> another, not made with hands." (Mark 14:58)

"In these days," writes Luke, Jesus "went out to the mountain
to pray, and all night he continued in prayer to God." This may well
have occurred more than a year into His ministry. Jesus spent all
night in prayer. The unusual construction of this phrase could be

translated "in the prayer of God." The purpose of this prayer session was concerning the choosing and calling of His apostles. Presumably, out of many who were following Jesus, He "chose from them twelve whom he named apostles" (Luke 6:13). The twelve were chosen here (Luke 6), but it is not until Luke 9:1 that they are officially commissioned. Twelve was not a random number. It was likely symbolic and connected to the twelve tribes of Israel. The appointment of a replacement after Judas's betrayal and death may say something about the importance of the number. The twelve were grouped into three sets of four. Simon Peter was always listed first, and Judas Iscariot was always last. In the four lists of the twelve, the groups remain the same, but the order within each group varies. The groups seem to be in descending order of intimacy with Christ. The first group included two sets of brothers. As mentioned, Peter always was listed first in group one; Philip was always first in group two, and James, the son of Alphaeus, was always first in group three. The apostles were greatly blessed, but they were hardly refined when Jesus chose them. They were marked by a lack of spiritual understanding, a lack of humility, a lack of faith, and a lack of power. God would transform them to be the ones who would establish His church. Mark wrote that Jesus "called to him those whom he desired" (Mark 3:13). At the end of Jesus's ministry, He revealed in His prayer:

> I have manifested your name to the people whom you gave me out of the world. Yours they were, and you gave them to me, and they have kept your word... I am praying for them. I am not praying for the world but for those whom you have given me, for they are yours... While I was with them, I kept them in your name, which you have given me. I have guarded them, and not one of them has been lost except the son of destruction, that the Scripture might be fulfilled. (John 17:6, 9, 12)

Jesus chose the twelve that the Father had determined to give to Him. He always did the will of the Father.

The Gospels are full of illustrations of the training of the twelve. Jesus trained them about the cost of being a disciple, as He explained to them the death of John the Baptist (Matt. 14:1–14). He made it clear to them that it would take courage to rebuke sin. There can be ministry in death as well as in life. A life that ended in trouble or tragedy did not indicate the disapproval of God. As Jesus multiplied miracles before the twelve, He was teaching them. The feeding of the five thousand, for example, was in some sense a parable of the future mission of the church (Matt. 14:13–21; Mark 6:30–44; Luke 9:10–17; John 6:1–13). Christ's provision for a needy world was to be distributed by His disciples. What may appear to be totally inadequate to meet the need becomes more than enough when applied at Jesus's direction by His disciples. When Jesus walked on water, the account began with Jesus on the heights interceding for the struggling disciples below. The disciples were following His commands when they encountered the storm, reminding them (and us) that being in a storm was not necessarily a bad thing or a wrong thing. In the darkest part of the storm, Jesus came to His disciples (Matt. 14:22–33). This is true in the challenges of life now and looks ahead to the time of His return. At Caesarea Philippi, Jesus taught His disciples about the nature and purpose and success of that which He would build through them.

> I will build my church... The gates of hell shall not prevail against it... I will give you the keys to the kingdom. (Matt. 16:18–19)

In the midst of such instruction, it was also necessary to give corrective rebuke.

> From that time Jesus began to show his disciples that he must go to Jerusalem and suffer many things from the elders and chief priests and scribes, and be killed, and on the third day be

raised. And Peter took him aside and began to
rebuke him, saying, "Far be it from you, Lord!
This shall never happen to you." But he turned
and said to Peter, "Get behind me, Satan! You are
a hindrance to me. For you are not setting your
mind on the things of God, but on the things of
man." (Matt. 16:21–23)

Several times in the Gospels, Jesus made clear the cost of following Him. Matthew 16:24–27 is representative. He gave His disciples
a solemn reminder, "If anyone would come after me, let him deny
himself and take up his cross and follow me." Though His instruction
appeared at times paradoxical, "For whoever would save his life will
lose it, but whoever loses his life for my sake will find it," He explained
the eternal perspective and reminded them of their sure reward.

For what will it profit a man if he gains the whole
world and forfeits his soul? Or what shall a man
give in return for his soul?… For the Son of Man
is going to come with his angels in the glory of
his Father, and then he will repay each person
according to what he has done. (Matt. 16:26–27)

At one point late in His ministry, Jesus announced the myste-
rious prediction:

Truly, I say to you, there are some standing here
who will not taste death until they see the Son of
Man coming in his kingdom. (Matt. 16:28)

Immediately following this, Matthew recorded the transfiguration. It is important to see the transfiguration in light of what Peter
said about that event years later.

For we did not follow cleverly devised myths
when we made known to you the power and

coming of our Lord Jesus Christ, but we were eyewitnesses of his majesty. For when he received honor and glory from God the Father, and the voice was borne to him by the Majestic Glory, "This is my beloved Son, with whom I am well pleased," we ourselves heard this very voice borne from heaven, for we were with him on the holy mountain. (2 Pet. 1:16–18)

Peter's evaluation of this incredible experience on the mountain occupied a lesser place of importance than the written record of God's revelation.

And we have the prophetic word more fully confirmed, to which you will do well to pay attention as to a lamp shining in a dark place, until the day dawns and the morning star rises in your hearts, knowing this first of all, that no prophecy of Scripture comes from someone's own interpretation. For no prophecy was ever produced by the will of man, but men spoke from God as they were carried along by the Holy Spirit. (2 Pet. 1:19–21)

Peter and James and John were selected to see the Lord transfigured before them. As Jesus's majesty, His intrinsic glory, began to show through the veil of His flesh, Moses and Elijah appeared. It has been suggested that these two OT saints could be representative of the Law and the prophets. Moses was both a lawgiver and a lawbreaker. He desired to enter the promised land but was forbidden. He was now present in the place he was not allowed to go during his earthly life. It has also been suggested that Moses represents all who have died, and Elijah, all who would be alive at Jesus's coming. The subject of their conversation, however, was not His return. According to Luke,

> And behold, two men were talking with him, Moses and Elijah, who appeared in glory and spoke of his departure, which he was about to accomplish at Jerusalem. (Luke 9:30–31)

The focus of their discussion concerned the death of Christ.

Immediately after Peter made his foolish proposal, a voice was heard from heaven (Matt. 17:5–8). These disciples were to once again be presented with the truth that Jesus was the unique Son of God. This event certainly spoke of His authority as well as the Father's approval of His Son's ministry. This too was a rebuke of Peter's suggestion. Suffering must precede glory, both for the Lord and for His disciples (cf. 16:21–22 and 1 Pet. 4:13). The ministries of Moses (Law) and Elijah (the prophets) were complete, and the voice of the Son of God was to be henceforth their authority.

For the disciples, this was the fulfillment of Jesus's statement that some would see the King and the kingdom before they died (Matt. 16:28). The transfiguration was a display of the essential glory of Jesus. It was confirmation of the truth uttered a week before, "You are the Christ" (Matt. 16:16), and it would offset the perplexity that the announcement of His coming death brought to the disciples (16:21–23). The message was that there would be glory beyond the cross for Jesus and His followers.

For Jesus, this was a foretaste of the coming glory, as well as encouragement as He faced and endured the cross. The transfiguration was assurance that the mystery of the cross was understood by the saints in heaven (Moses and Elijah), even if those on earth failed to understand. The approving voice of the Father was assurance that Jesus pleased His Father in His ministry up to that point, and it served as advance approval of what He was about to accomplish. Some confusion remained in the minds of the disciples regarding Elijah (Matt. 17:9–10). They wondered why Elijah had not come down the mountain with them since he was to be the messenger of the coming Messiah according to the prophet Malachi.

> Behold, I send my messenger, and he will pre-pare the way before me. And the Lord whom you seek will suddenly come to his temple; and the messenger of the covenant in whom you delight, behold, he is coming, says the LORD of hosts... Behold, I will send you Elijah the prophet before the great and awesome day of the LORD comes. And he will turn the hearts of fathers to their chil-dren and the hearts of children to their fathers, lest I come and strike the land with a decree of utter destruction. (Mal. 3:1; 4:5–6)

The explanation for their concern was answered by the Lord:

> Elijah does come, and he will restore all things. But I tell you that Elijah has already come, and they did not recognize him, but did to him what-ever they pleased. So also the Son of Man will certainly suffer at their hands. (Matt. 17:11–12).

Matthew concluded, "Then the disciples understood that he was speaking to them of John the Baptist" (Matt. 17:13).

Even as the disciples were being trained and taught, evidence of the rejection of the Messiah was growing. Matthew 11 and 12 mark a pivotal time in the ministry of Jesus. There was a change in His teaching after these events. Jesus had been offering Himself as the King, promised by the prophets. The clear offer as King to the mul-titudes changed to teaching in parables, and the audience changed from large crowds to the twelve. At this time, John the Baptist was in prison. Some of John's disciples had come to Jesus to find out, for their beloved leader, John, if Jesus was the one promised or if they should look for another. John had heard of the healing of many but judgment to none, so he wondered if Jesus was really the Messiah to come. The kingdom, since the beginning of Jesus's ministry, had been advancing, but not all of the opposition had been eliminated, as John had expected. To explain, Jesus used the illustration of children at play. The application was something like, "You would not have John; you won't have Me. You are bound to have your own way." Like disgruntled children, that generation found it easier to criticize and voice discontent than to "play the game."

Some of the most severe words of judgment uttered by the Lord were followed by some of the most sensitive. Matthew 11 concluded with a prayer, a declaration, and an invitation. We get a glimpse of the relationship between Jesus and the Father and some insight into how the Father was revealed.

> No one knows the Son except the Father, and no one knows the Father except the Son and anyone to whom the Son chooses to reveal to him. (Matt. 11:27)

To those who knew the Father and the Son, the invitation was given to "Come...take...learn...find" (Matt. 11:28–29).

As Jesus continued to teach in the midst of growing hostility, He used parables to discriminate between believers and determined unbelievers (Luke 8:10; Matt. 13:10–15). The teachings of the parables of the kingdom recorded in Matthew 13 were given the same day that Jesus warned the Pharisees in regard to the "unpardonable sin." The twofold purpose for the use of parables was stated in Matthew 13:11–13. Those who were willing, by faith, to receive the truth were enlightened, but those who had rejected the truth were further blinded. Teaching in parables fulfilled Isaiah's prophecy (Isa. 6:9–10; Matt. 13:14–15). Israel, as a nation, had rejected her King and the kingdom. Additional truth would be hidden from them as judgment against them. The same truth that would enlighten some would harden others. The apostle Paul would make this same argument in regard to Israel's blindness to the Gospel (Rom. 11:25). Refusing to believe became inability to believe. In effect, the use of parables became a sort of preliminary judgment against those who rejected Christ.

An example of Jesus's parabolic teaching method is the parable of the sower. There is little room for misinterpretation here because Jesus explained the meaning to His disciples, and that explanation was recorded. The four types of soil illustrated four conditions of the heart. The first condition, the hard heart, was naturally hardened by the walk of life. When the seed, the Word of God, was scattered on the hard soil, it was picked clean by the god of this world. Paul explained,

> In such case the god of this world has blinded the minds of the unbelieving, that they might not see the light of the gospel of the glory of Christ, who is the image of God. (2 Cor. 4:4)

Satan will use any means, doubt, prejudice, stubbornness, procrastination, love of the world, love of sin, or any combination of these and others to snatch away the seed. When the seed is taken away, there will be no fruit.

The shallow heart illustrated the initial positive response of some toward the Word. But what appeared to be green and alive one day was withered and brown the next. The seed was good, the sower was faithful, the soil looked ready, but just underneath the surface was a layer of stone. The seedling seemed to begin well, but nothing became of it. When the sun came out, which was necessary to produce growth, it caused the little plant to burn up. There was no fruit. When God prepares the soil, He cleans out the weeds. He forgives the sin, and He provides the Holy Spirit who points out any new weeds that need to be pulled. The heart, in other words, is prepared to bear fruit. If the heart is not prepared, the seed will be choked, and soon the heart will be more weed infested than it was at the beginning. It is the nature of our unregenerate hearts to yield weeds. If the soil is not prepared, there will be no fruit. But when the heart is prepared by the Lord Himself and the good seed is planted, it will yield much fruit.

Good seed on hard soil provides food for the enemy. Good seed on shallow soil produces short-term promise but no fruit. Good seed on crowded soil is swallowed up and overwhelmed, never yielding even one additional seed. Good seed on prepared ground produces genuine fruit. God is able to break up hard hearts and make then soft. He is able to deepen shallow hearts and make them ready to receive His Word. He is able to take the crowded heart and clear away the thorns and thistles, the cares, and the temporal value systems and make the soil ready to receive the good seed, bearing good fruit. In fact, He must do this if there is to be genuine fruit.

Each Gospel writer, in his own way, under the sovereign direction and protection of the Holy Spirit, recorded the closing days of Jesus earthly life before His crucifixion. In Luke's Gospel, we are given the revelation of God concerning Jesus's triumphal entry into the city of Jerusalem where He effectively presented Himself as the promised Messiah.

> And when he had said these things, he went on ahead, going up to Jerusalem. When he drew near to Bethphage and Bethany, at the mount that is called Olivet, he sent two of the disciples, saying, "Go into the village in front of you, where on entering you will find a colt tied, on which no one has ever yet sat. Untie it and bring it here. If anyone asks you, 'Why are you untying it?' you shall say this: 'The Lord has need of it.'" So those who were sent went away and found it just as he had told them. And as they were untying the colt, its owners said to them, "Why are you untying the colt?" And they said, "The Lord has need of it." And they brought it to Jesus, and throwing their cloaks on the colt, they set Jesus on it. (Luke 19:28–35)

According to Matthew, part of this event reflected a "prophetic necessity."

> This took place to fulfill what was spoken by the prophet, saying, "Say to the daughter of Zion,

> 'Behold, your king is coming to you, humble, and mounted on a donkey, on a colt, the foal of a beast of burden.'" (Matt. 21:4–5)

The OT source of the quotation was Zechariah 9:9.

> Rejoice greatly, O daughter of Zion! Shout aloud, O daughter of Jerusalem! Behold, your king is coming to you; righteous and having salvation is he, humble and mounted on a donkey, on a colt, the foal of a donkey.

Luke wrote,

> Most of the crowd spread their cloaks on the road, and others cut branches from the trees and spread them on the road. (Luke 19:36)

And John added,

> So they took branches of palm trees and went out to meet him, crying out, "Hosanna! Blessed is he who comes in the name of the Lord, even the King of Israel!" (John 12:13)

The strewing of clothing and palm branches were an act reserved for high-ranking dignitaries. The crowd was giving Jesus the highest honor possible. The reason for the acclaim was "for all the mighty works that they had seen" (Luke 19:37). Matthew wrote,

> And the crowds that went before him and that followed him were shouting, "Hosanna to the Son of David! Blessed is he who comes in the name of the Lord! Hosanna in the highest!" (Matt. 21:10)

And Mark added, "Blessed is the coming kingdom of our father David! Hosanna in the highest!" (Mark 11:10). This was the language of Psalm 118, recognized by the Jews as one of the greatest Messianic psalms recorded. Portions of the Psalm include,

> Open to me the gates of righteousness, that I may enter through them and give thanks to the LORD. This is the gate of the LORD; the righteous shall enter through it. I thank you that you have answered me and have become my salvation. The stone that the builders rejected has become the cornerstone. This is the LORD's doing; it is marvelous in our eyes. This is the day that the LORD has made; let us rejoice and be glad in it. Save us, we pray, O LORD! O LORD, we pray, give us success! Blessed is he who comes in the name of the LORD! We bless you from the house of the LORD. The LORD is God, and he has made his light to shine upon us. Bind the festal sacrifice with cords, up to the horns of the altar! (Ps. 118:19–27)

The Pharisees strongly objected, "Teacher, rebuke your disciples." He answered, "I tell you, if these were silent, the very stones would cry out" (Luke 19:39–40). Jesus's response to their demand made clear that something had changed in His ministry. The Pharisees' objection would culminate in murder, but even killing Jesus would not silence the message. Luke continued with Jesus's lamentation over the city.

> And when he drew near and saw the city, he wept over it, saying, "Would that you, even you, had known on this day the things that make for peace! But now they are hidden from your eyes. For the days will come upon you, when your enemies will set up a barricade around you and surround you and hem you in on every side and tear

you down to the ground, you and your children within you. And they will not leave one stone upon another in you, because you did not know the time of your visitation." (Luke 19:41–44)

Jesus wept over the city though He knew the people would reject Him and kill Him. He also knew where this would eventually lead in relation to Jerusalem's destruction in less than forty years! Luke provided prophetic time notations such as "on this day" (verse 41) and "the days will come" (verse 43), and "the time of your visitation" (verse 44). The prophet Daniel had prophesied of the day when Messiah would arrive in Jerusalem.

> Know therefore and understand that from the going out of the word to restore and build Jerusalem to the *coming of an anointed one*, a prince, there shall be seven weeks. Then for sixty-two weeks it shall be built again with squares and moat, but in a troubled time. And after the sixty-two weeks, *an anointed one shall be cut off* and shall have nothing. And the people of the prince who is to come shall destroy the city and the sanctuary. Its end shall come with a flood, and to the end there shall be war. Desolations are decreed. And he shall make a strong covenant with many for one week, and for half of the week he shall put an end to sacrifice and offering. And on the wing of abominations shall come one who makes desolate, until the decreed end is poured out on the desolator. (Dan. 9:25–27; emphasis added).

This was not a random day but a day set in eternity past to begin the fulfillment of the plan of God in regard to the Messiah's atoning sacrifice. This triumphal entry was the Messiah's official offer of Himself as the King of Israel. The offer was confirmed as Jesus entered the temple and drove out those who were selling.

> "It is written, 'My house shall be a house of prayer,' but you have made it a den of robbers." And he was teaching daily in the temple. (Luke 19:46–47)

The King was laying claim to the temple as His house, fulfilling the prophetic words of Malachi:

> Behold, I send my messenger, and he will prepare the way before me. And the Lord whom you seek will suddenly come to his temple; and the messenger of the covenant in whom you delight, behold, he is coming, says the LORD of hosts. (Mal. 3:1)

In capsule form, what Jesus did here was a picture of the blessings to be present during His reign. All of this was pointing to the time when Israel, with a contrite heart, would recognize and receive the Messiah as prophesied by Isaiah.

> It will be said on that day, "Behold, this is our God; we have waited for him, that he might save us. This is the LORD; we have waited for him; let us be glad and rejoice in his salvation." (Isa. 25:9)

The prophet had declared that the Word would go forth from Jerusalem.

> It shall come to pass in the latter days that the mountain of the house of the LORD shall be established as the highest of the mountains, and shall be lifted up above the hills; and all the nations shall flow to it, and many peoples shall come, and say: "Come, let us go up to the mountain

of the LORD, to the house of the God of Jacob, that he may teach us his ways and that we may walk in his paths." For out of Zion shall go the law, and the word of the LORD from Jerusalem. (Isa. 2:2–3)

Many other OT prophecies were connected to Jesus's coming to Jerusalem. A sample of healing from the King on all with physical affliction as described in Isaiah 35:4–6 was given by Jesus here.

Say to those who have an anxious heart, "Be strong; fear not! Behold, your God will come with vengeance, with the recompense of God. He will come and save you." Then the eyes of the blind shall be opened, and the ears of the deaf unstopped; then shall the lame man leap like a deer, and the tongue of the mute sing for joy. For waters break forth in the wilderness, and streams in the desert.

The foretaste of blessing was accompanied by a foretaste of judgment. Ezekiel prophesied of the day when God would cast out the greedy shepherds of Israel.

Because my shepherds have not searched for my sheep, but the shepherds have fed themselves, and have not fed my sheep, therefore, you shepherds, hear the word of the LORD: Thus says the Lord GOD, Behold, I am against the shepherds, and I will require my sheep at their hand and put a stop to their feeding the sheep. No longer shall the shepherds feed themselves. I will rescue my sheep from their mouths, that they may not be food for them. (Ezek. 34:8–10)

The children crying out, "Hosanna," were unknowingly acting out the words of the psalmist recorded in Psalm 8:

> O LORD, our Lord, how majestic is your name in all the earth! You have set your glory above the heavens. Out of the mouth of babies and infants, you have established strength because of your foes, to still the enemy and the avenger. (Ps. 8:1–2)

But the religious leaders of the day failed to make the OT connection. They would have none of this.

> The chief priests and the scribes and the principal men of the people were seeking to destroy him, but they did not find anything they could do, for all the people were hanging on his words. (Luke 19:47–48)

Their only solution was to find a way to kill Jesus!

Between the triumphal entry and the crucifixion, Matthew provided insight into the future of Jerusalem as he recorded Jesus's discourse to His disciples from the Mount of Olives (Matt. 24–25). Jesus and His disciples had been in Jerusalem at the temple mount. For some reason, the disciples were pointing out the structures, which prompted Jesus to say, "You see all these, do you not? Truly, I say to you, there will not be left here one stone upon another that will not be thrown down" (Matt. 24:2). Jesus spoke of birth pains (24:4–14), Daniel's "abomination of desolation" (24:15), perils to come (24:16–28), the sign of the Son of Man (24:29–31), information regarding the final generation (24:32–35), information regarding His coming in judgment (24:36–51), a parable outlining the fate of the unprepared (25:1–13), and finally, the tragedy of wasted opportunity (25:14–30).

The apostle John took a different approach than the synoptics, with the revelation of an extended discourse to the disciples as they were gathered in a prepared upper chamber to observe the Passover feast. This was merely hours before the crucifixion. Jesus began the instruction with a lesson in humility as He washed each of the disciple's feet (John 13). The encounter with Peter is instructive. Jesus announced that one among them would betray Him. Soon after, Judas left the assembly. Jesus instructed the remaining disciples concerning the "new commandment" to love one another. John 13 ends with Peter's response to Jesus's words, "Where I am going you cannot come" (John 13:36). Peter declared his loyalty even to the point of laying down his life for Jesus. Jesus responded, "Will you lay down your life for me? Truly, truly, I say to you, the rooster will not crow until you have denied me three times" (John 13:38).

This discourse continued through chapter 16. In chapter 14, Jesus dealt with the troubled hearts of His followers, promising them they would be with Him in the Father's house but that no one could come to the Father except through Him. Both Thomas and Philip responded. Jesus announced that though He was leaving, He was sending "another Helper" (John 14:16), the Holy Spirit, who would be with them forever. He promised, in effect, a Trinitarian occupation of all who would believe. He announced at the end of chapter 14 that it was time to depart. Chapter 15 records what perhaps occurred as Jesus and His disciples were on their way to the Mount of Olives, as Jesus taught the disciples about the vine and the branches, calling them to "bear much fruit and so prove to be my disciples" (John 15:8). Additional instruction was given in regard to the Holy Spirit.

In Chapter 16, Jesus gave instructions regarding the work of the coming Holy Spirit. He also gave some indication about the future recording of the revelation of God.

> I still have many things to say to you, but you cannot bear them now. When the Spirit of truth comes, he will guide you into all the truth, for he will not speak on his own authority, but whatever he hears he will speak, and he will declare to you the things that are to come. He will glorify me, for he will take what is mine and declare it to you. All that the Father has is mine; therefore, I

said that he will take what is mine and declare it to you. (John 16:12–15)

Jesus also spoke of the sorrow the disciples would experience, but He promised them,

> I will see you again, and your hearts will rejoice, and no one will take your joy from you. In that day you will ask nothing of me. Truly, truly, I say to you, whatever you ask of the Father in my name, he will give it to you. Until now you have asked nothing in my name. Ask, and you will receive, that your joy may be full. (John 16:22–24)

John 17 contains the prayer of Jesus to the Father. Where and exactly when this was prayed we are not told. Jesus spoke of glory, both His and the Father's glory. He prayed for Himself and then for His disciples, and finally for all future disciples.

> While I was with them, I kept them in your name, which you have given me. I have guarded them, and not one of them has been lost except the son of destruction, that the Scripture might be fulfilled. But now I am coming to you, and these things I speak in the world, that they may have my joy fulfilled in themselves. I have given them your word, and the world has hated them because they are not of the world, just as I am not of the world. I do not ask that you take them out of the world, but that you keep them from the evil one. They are not of the world, just as I am not of the world. Sanctify them in the truth; your word is truth. As you sent me into the world, so I have sent them into the world. And for their sake I consecrate myself, that they also may be

sanctified in truth. I do not ask for these only, but also for those who will believe in me through their word. (John 17:12–20)[9]

With Jesus's arrival at the garden in the olive grove, the magnitude of what was about to happen was introduced. Matthew wrote,

> Then he said to them, "My soul is very sorrowful, even to death; remain here, and watch with me." And going a little farther he fell on his face and prayed, saying, "My Father, if it be possible, let this cup pass from me; nevertheless, not as I will, but as you will." And he came to the disciples and found them sleeping. And he said to Peter, "So, could you not watch with me one hour? Watch and pray that you may not enter into temptation. The spirit indeed is willing, but the flesh is weak." Again, for the second time, he went away and prayed, "My Father, if this cannot pass unless I drink it, your will be done." And again he came and found them sleeping, for their eyes were heavy. So, leaving them again, he went away and prayed for the third time, saying the same words again. Then he came to the disciples and said to them, "Sleep and take your rest later on. See, the hour is at hand, and the Son of Man is betrayed into the hands of sinners. Rise, let us be going; see, my betrayer is at hand." (Matt. 26:38–46)

As the mob arrived, Judas came forward and betrayed Jesus with a kiss. Jesus's words to Judas are surprising, "Friend, do what you came

---

9. When the author of Hebrews wrote, "In these last days he has spoken to us by his Son," that includes what Jesus has spoken through the apostles who recorded the NT. Note that He prayed, for those who would believe in Him, through "their word." "Their word" was the recording of His Word.

to do" (Matt. 26:50). Peter pulled out a sword, cutting off the ear of a servant of the high priest. Jesus was quick to rebuke His disciple:

> "Put your sword back into its place. For all who take the sword will perish by the sword. Do you think that I cannot appeal to my Father, and he will at once send me more than twelve legions of angels? But how then should the Scriptures be fulfilled, that it must be so?" At that hour Jesus said to the crowds, "Have you come out as against a robber, with swords and clubs to capture me? Day after day I sat in the temple teaching, and you did not seize me. But all this has taken place that the Scriptures of the prophets might be fulfilled." (Matt. 26:52–56).

The Lord Jesus was forcefully taken from the garden and brought before the high priest for the first of several trials. Before Caiaphas, Jesus was silent (Matt. 26:63). When the high priest demanded that He tell whether or not He was the Christ, Jesus answered, "You have said so. But I tell you, from now on you will see the Son of Man seated at the right hand of Power and coming on the clouds of heaven" (Matt. 26:54). Jesus was then taken before Pilate. Pilate asked, "Are you the king of the Jews?" Jesus answered, "You have said so" (Matt. 27:11). But before the chief priest and the elders, "he gave no answer" (Matt. 27:12). When Pilate asked Jesus if He heard how many charges they had brought against Him, "he gave no answer, not even to a single charge" (Matt. 27:14). Pilate was amazed. Luke mentioned Jesus before the council and also before Herod. Herod "questioned him at some length, but he made no answer" (Luke 23:9). Having no more use for Jesus, Herod sent Him back to Pilate (Luke 23:11), who eventually delivered Jesus over to the will of those who were calling for His crucifixion. Jesus was led away and crucified.

The words of Jesus from the cross are well known. The first was a cry for pardon, "Father, forgive them, for they know not what they do" (Luke 23:34). The second utterance of the Lord Jesus was to the repentant thief who hung beside Him: "Truly I say to you, today you will be with me in Paradise" (Luke 23:43). John recorded Jesus's compassionate words directed to His closest disciple and to Mary, His earthly mother.

> When Jesus saw his mother and the disciple whom he loved standing nearby, he said to his mother, "Woman, behold, your son!" Then he said to the disciple, "Behold, your mother!" And from that hour the disciple took her to his own home. (John 19:26–27)

Just before His death, Jesus uttered His final four statements from the cross. As Jesus endured the wrath of a holy God against Him as He bore the sins of the world, He cried in anguish, "Eli, Eli, lema sabachthani?" which means, "My God, my God, why have you forsaken me?" Matthew indicated that this happened about the ninth hour, about three in the afternoon (Matt. 27:46). The next declaration from the cross indicated His suffering but also His determination to be heard: "I thirst" (John 19:28), followed almost immediately with, "It is finished" (John 19:30). This was not only a cry announcing the completion of His work on the cross, but a cry of victory. Luke records the final statement:

> Then Jesus, calling out with a loud voice, said, "Father, into your hands I commit my spirit!" And having said this he breathed his last. (Luke 23:46)

The recorded words of Jesus did not end with, "Father, into your hands I commit my spirit!" The Gospels and the Acts record several post-resurrection announcements, post-resurrection appearances. and the ascension of Jesus to heaven. The announcement regarding Jesus's resurrection was first made by angels to the women who had come to the tomb (Matt. 28, Mark 16, and Luke 24). Jesus appeared to Mary Magdalene and to other women (Mark 16:9). These women had come to the tomb presumably to properly prepare the body of Jesus, perhaps assuming that Joseph and Nicodemus had not properly completed the task. When they arrived, they found the tomb open and empty. Matthew recorded that

> They departed quickly from the tomb with fear
> and great joy and ran to tell his disciples. And
> behold, Jesus met them and said, "Greetings!"
> And they came up and took hold of his feet and
> worshiped him. Then Jesus said to them, "Do not
> be afraid; go and tell my brothers to go to Galilee,
> and there they will see me." (Matt. 28:8–10)

On the evening of the resurrection, Jesus appeared to an Emmaus couple returning home from Jerusalem (Luke 24:13–35). This encounter and conversation are significant for our consideration in relation to what Jesus said regarding the OT Scriptures and Himself. The couple shared their experience with Jesus, though they did not recognize Him.

> But we had hoped that he was the one to redeem
> Israel. Yes, and besides all this, it is now the third
> day since these things happened. Moreover, some
> women of our company amazed us. They were at
> the tomb early in the morning, and when they
> did not find his body, they came back saying
> that they had even seen a vision of angels, who
> said that he was alive. Some of those who were
> with us went to the tomb and found it just as
> the women had said, but him they did not see.
> And he said to them, "O foolish ones, and slow
> of heart to believe all that the prophets have spo-
> ken! Was it not necessary that the Christ should
> suffer these things and enter into his glory?"
> And beginning with Moses and all the Prophets,
> he interpreted to them in all the Scriptures the

things concerning himself. So they drew near to the village to which they were going. He acted as if he were going farther, but they urged him strongly, saying, "Stay with us, for it is toward evening and the day is now far spent." So he went in to stay with them. When he was at table with them, he took the bread and blessed and broke it and gave it to them. And their eyes were opened, and they recognized him. And he vanished from their sight. They said to each other, "Did not our hearts burn within us while he talked to us on the road, while he opened to us the Scriptures?" And they rose that same hour and returned to Jerusalem. And they found the eleven and those who were with them gathered together, saying, "The Lord has risen indeed, and has appeared to Simon!" Then they told what had happened on the road, and how he was known to them in the breaking of the bread. (Luke 24:21–35)

Later that evening, Jesus appeared to ten of the apostles and others.

As they were talking about these things, Jesus himself stood among them, and said to them, "Peace to you!" But they were startled and frightened and thought they saw a spirit. And he said to them, "Why are you troubled, and why do doubts arise in your hearts? See my hands and my feet, that it is I myself. Touch me and see. For a spirit does not have flesh and bones as you see that I have." And when he had said this, he showed them his hands and his feet. And while they still disbelieved for joy and were marveling, he said to them, "Have you anything here to eat?" They gave him a piece of broiled fish,

and he took it and ate before them. Then he said
to them, "These are my words that I spoke to
you while I was still with you, that everything
written about me in the Law of Moses and the
Prophets and the Psalms must be fulfilled,"
Then he opened their minds to understand the
Scriptures, and said to them, "Thus it is written,
that the Christ should suffer and on the third day
rise from the dead, and that repentance for the
forgiveness of sins should be proclaimed in his
name to all nations, beginning from Jerusalem.
You are witnesses of these things. And behold, I
am sending the promise of my Father upon you.
But stay in the city until you are clothed with
power from on high." (Luke 24:36–49)

A week later, Jesus appeared again to His disciples, and this time
Thomas was present. Jesus's message to him had significance in relation to trusting who He was by what He had said.

Eight days later, his disciples were inside again,
and Thomas was with them. Although the doors
were locked, Jesus came and stood among them
and said, "Peace be with you." Then he said
to Thomas, "Put your finger here, and see my
hands; and put out your hand and place it in my
side. Do not disbelieve, but believe." Thomas
answered him, "My Lord and my God!" Jesus
said to him, "Have you believed because you have
seen me? Blessed are those who have not seen and
yet have believed." (John 20:26–29)

In John 21, Jesus made another appearance to some of the disciples at the Sea of Galilee. While He was still unrecognized, He asked
them, "Children, do you have any fish?" Hearing that they had none,
He instructed them to "cast the net on the right side of the boat, and you

will find some." After eating the breakfast that He had prepared, Jesus spoke to Peter, "Simon, son of John, do you love me more than these?" That question was asked three times, and Peter each time answered affirmatively. Jesus gave essentially the same charge to each of Peter's answers—"Feed my sheep." Jesus then gave this prophetic word to Peter:

> "Truly, truly, I say to you, when you were young, you used to dress yourself and walk wherever you wanted, but when you are old, you will stretch out your hands, and another will dress you and carry you where you do not want to go." (This he said to show by what kind of death he was to glorify God.) And after saying this he said to him, "Follow me." (John 21:18–19)

Peter, seeing John, asked, "What about this man?" Jesus answered, "If it is my will that he remain until I come, what is that to you? You follow me!" (John 21:21–22).

There were also specific appearances to Peter and also to a group of five hundred brothers, according to 1 Corinthians 15:5–6. However, the content of Jesus's conversations was not recorded. It appears that all of Jesus's post-resurrection appearances were to believers. Matthew provided the final Gospel account of Jesus's words as He was about to ascend into heaven.

> Now the eleven disciples went to Galilee, to the mountain to which Jesus had directed them. And when they saw him they worshiped him, but some doubted. And Jesus came and said to them, "All authority in heaven and on earth has been given to me. Go therefore and make disciples of all nations, baptizing them in the name of the Father and of the Son and of the Holy Spirit, teaching them to observe all that I have commanded you. And behold, I am with you always, to the end of the age." (Matt. 28:16–20)

The ascension account from Luke is less detailed.

> And he led them out as far as Bethany and lifting
> up his hands he blessed them. While he blessed
> them, he parted from them and was carried up
> into heaven. (Luke 24:50–51)

However, Luke provided additional words from Jesus at the beginning of Acts.

> So when they had come together, they asked him,
> "Lord, will you at this time restore the kingdom
> to Israel?" He said to them, "It is not for you to
> know times or seasons that the Father has fixed
> by his own authority. But you will receive power
> when the Holy Spirit has come upon you, and
> you will be my witnesses in Jerusalem and in all
> Judea and Samaria, and to the end of the earth."
> And when he had said these things, as they were
> looking on, he was lifted up, and a cloud took
> him out of their sight. (Acts 1:6–9)

To conclude our consideration of God speaking through His Son, about half of the four Gospels are the record of the words of Jesus, direct quotations from His conversations. The remaining half of the Gospel record are words of Matthew, Mark, Luke, and John providing the setting, the conversations of others reacting and responding to Jesus, as well as commentary on what Jesus said and did—but in its entirety, inspired text, clearly written by these four writers, but carried along by the Holy Spirit, so that what was written was revelation from God Himself.

When Jesus spoke, He spoke as the Son of God, which, defined by John, meant to be equal with God (John 5:18). The differences in God speaking in the OT and God speaking in NT are significant. When God spoke in the OT, generally God's words came to a prophet, and those words came through dreams or visions. If God spoke directly to the prophet (such as to Moses), it was a voice or perhaps an angelic being delivering the message. In the case of the angel of the Lord, it was God Himself who gave the revelation, though He appeared as an angel. Such appearances were few and brief. After the message was communicated, the angel of the Lord would disappear. Jesus, however, in the NT, was human in every aspect, except without sin, but He was also perfectly God. For more than thirty years, He lived among people who never had any question about His humanity. For three plus years of ministry, Jesus walked among people and taught people who were able to stand in His presence and live, because He was "veiled in human flesh." Though most of these people did not recognize Him as God, He was God, speaking the revelation of God. John would declare Him to be "the Word of God."

In Jesus's resurrection appearances to the Emmaus couple and to His disciples, He demonstrated that the OT was essentially about Him. As the author of Hebrews explained, that revelation came through prophets. The Gospels obviously are about Jesus because the Gospel writers recorded His words as He spoke directly to many. The remainder of the NT is also about the Lord Jesus explaining His work of building His church. The NT culminates in the prophetic record of His return in glory!

The author of Hebrews, speaking about God the Father, said,

> But in these last days he has spoken to us by his Son, whom he appointed the heir of all things, through whom also he created the world. He is the radiance of the glory of God and the exact imprint of his nature, and he upholds the universe by the word of his power. (Heb. 1:2–3)

The second person of the triune God spoke the universe into existence; He upholds that universe by His powerful word, and in these Gospel accounts, He spoke words of life to people who did not know that God was present with them!

The Acts of the Apostles, the Epistles, and the Revelation

Unlike the books of prophecy and the direct accounts of our Lord speaking in the Gospels, the remainder of the NT is more of a commentary on those accounts. There are still significant quotations from the OT, and there are certainly ample reasons to believe that the remaining books, the book of Acts through the book of Revelation, are inspired by God as part of the canon of Scripture.

In the words of the last book of the canon, there seems to be a finality to the record of God speaking. The prophetic content of Revelation takes us to the time when the Son of God will return in power and great glory. This present age is not silent like those years between the Testaments, however. The saints after Malachi were waiting for God to complete the story of His coming. Although they had the OT prophets, there remained gaps in their understanding that they were unable to bridge. But when Jesus came, and the apostles wrote of His incarnation, they made clear that the revelation of God was as complete as it was intended to be until the end of the age.

> This is now the second letter that I am writing to you, beloved. In both of them I am stirring up your sincere mind by way of reminder, that you should remember the predictions of the holy prophets and the commandment of the Lord and Savior through your apostles. (2 Pet. 3:1–2)

The Acts of the Apostles opens with a promise of the coming Spirit, the ascension of Jesus, and the choosing of Matthias as the replacement apostle for Judas Iscariot. According to Luke, Jesus appeared to the apostles during the forty days between His resurrection and His ascension. He was "speaking about the kingdom of God." Luke writes, "While staying with them, he ordered them not to depart from Jerusalem but to wait for the promise of the Father" (Acts 1:3–4). It is not likely that Jesus remained with His apostles constantly throughout the forty days. He appeared from time to time. "While staying with them" probably indicates that the message they received, recorded here, was received while He remained on earth prior to His ascension.

Included were reminders of earlier promises Jesus had made to His apostles. They continued to be interested in knowing the time that Jesus would establish His kingdom. He briefly answered their question that it was not for them to know, indicating that they would not be receiving any revelation to answer the "when" question. He did again speak in Acts 1:8 of the coming of the Spirit. As Jesus ascended out of sight, two angels appeared, promising that as He departed, so He would return.

Luke provided some insight on the demise of Judas, which opened the question as to a possible successor. Peter, as spokesperson for the group, appealed to the OT Scripture for the justification to recognize another apostle. Quotations from the Psalms were cited as the fulfillment of prophecy in regard to Judas and also the need for a replacement. That was done through prayer and the casting of lots (1:24–26). Rather than wait for a fresh revelatory word from God in whatever form, the OT Scripture was considered, and the choice of Matthias was left to the providence of God through the casting of lots.

The apostles waited in Jerusalem for the promised Holy Spirit. The fulfillment of Jesus's promise came on the day of Pentecost. Clearly something new was happening, and it was accompanied by signs. This was the answer to the promise given by Jesus of the coming of the Holy Spirit. Peter seized the occasion to preach to the crowd. His sermon texts included selections from Joel 2, Psalm 16, and Psalm 110. The response of the people to Peter's sermon was, "Brothers, what shall we do?" (Acts 2:37). They were called to repent of their sin and to affirm their faith by identifying with Jesus in baptism (2:38). Three thousand people were added that day to the group of believers.[10]

Peter was the primary character through roughly half of the book of Acts. He and John ministered together in chapters 3 and 4. There seem to be examples of the fulfillment of the promise of Jesus that when His disciples were dragged before others, that the Holy Spirit would give them utterance (Luke 12:12, compare with Acts 4:8, 31). The evidence of the presence and work of the Spirit was seen in the believers' boldness in speaking the Word of God. Presumably this was the preaching of the OT Scriptures in light of the death and resurrection of Jesus. The Spirit was granting illumination to the OT texts.

In Acts 5, Peter seemed to have been given revelation from God concerning the lie that came from Ananias and Sapphira. Later, after the apostles had been put into a public prison (5:18), an angel of the Lord came to them, opened the prison doors, and delivered to them revelation from God to go and stand in the temple and speak to the people the words of life (5:20). In the next chapter, a dispute arose regarding the feeding of widows. The solution seemed to be determined by the collective wisdom of the apostles rather than any direct revelation from God. In chapter 7, as Stephen concluded his sermon, quoting numerous texts from the OT, he saw "the glory of God and Jesus standing at the right hand of God" (7:55). This was a special revelatory vision for Stephen as he was being martyred. In chapter 8, Philip was given revelation from an angel (vv. 26, 29). It is important to note that the message Philip had for the Ethiopian was from the OT Scriptures (v. 35). In Acts 10, Peter was given revelation through a vision regarding God's intention to extend salvation to the Gentiles. The Gentiles received the same sign as the Jews at salvation, marking what they had received as a genuine salvific work of God.

[10.] See the previous notes on Joel on pages 102–103.

The apostle James had been killed by Herod, and Peter had been arrested with the intent that he too would be killed with the sword (Acts 12). Of course, that was not to happen according to the prophecy Jesus had given to Peter about his death (John 21:18). Whether Peter remembered that or not, we do not know. Nevertheless, he was able to sleep as he laid in a prison cell between two guards awaiting the outcome the next morning. Peter was awakened by an angel and miraculously led out of prison and given instructions.

The remainder of the Acts is dominated by the apostle Paul. Chapter 9 recorded Paul's encounter with Jesus. Jesus spoke to Paul, though Paul was at this time unable to see. Others with Paul also heard the voice from heaven (9:7). Jesus gave Saul instructions. The Lord also spoke to a disciple in Damascus, named Ananias, and gave him instructions regarding Saul. Ananias balked, knowing Saul's reputation, but the Lord spoke reassurance:

> Go, for he is a chosen instrument of mine to carry my name before the Gentiles and kings and the children of Israel. For I will show him how much he must suffer for the sake of my name. (Acts 9:15–16)

The account of Paul's conversion was restated in chapters 22 and 26.

Chapters 13 through 21 outline Paul's missionary endeavors. Chapter 15 is the record of the meeting of a council in Jerusalem to decide how Jewish believers were to respond to Gentiles turning, in faith, to the Lord Jesus. Any directives in relation to the proclamation of the Gospel were more providential than revelatory (16:7). One significant departure from that might be the "Macedonian Call" in Acts 16. It came as a vision in the night (16:9–10). One other such departure is recorded in chapter 18, when the Lord spoke to Paul in a vision:

> Do not be afraid, but go on speaking and do not be silent, for I am with you, and no one will

attack you to harm you, for I have many in this
city who are my people. (Acts 18:9–10)

This prophetic message was to encourage Paul to remain in
Corinth and to continue preaching. God had others there that He
would draw to Himself.

In chapter 21 we are introduced to Philip's four unmarried
prophetess daughters and a prophet named Agabus. The role of NT
prophets may or may not have been the same as the role of OT prophets, but regarding the revelatory work of God, God was now speaking
mostly to the apostles rather than to NT prophets. In other words,
in regard to canonical revelation, most came through the apostles.

In chapter 27, with Paul as a prisoner on a ship headed for
Rome, the ship encountered a hurricane. Paul received a vision from
an angel of God promising that every life on the ship would be
spared, but the ship itself would be destroyed.

> For this very night there stood before me an angel
> of the God to whom I belong and whom I wor-
> ship, and he said, "Do not be afraid, Paul; you
> must stand before Caesar. And behold, God has
> granted you all those who sail with you." So take
> heart, men, for I have faith in God that it will
> be exactly as I have been told. But we must run
> aground on some island. (Acts 27:23–26)

The vision the apostle Paul received was reminiscent of the
visions seen in the OT directed to the prophets.

The book of Acts concludes with,

> "Therefore let it be known to you that this salva-
> tion of God has been sent to the Gentiles; they
> will listen." He lived there two whole years at his
> own expense, and welcomed all who came to him,
> proclaiming the kingdom of God and teaching

about the Lord Jesus Christ with all boldness and without hindrance. (28:28–31)

The apostle Paul's epistles are primarily instruction, coming from the Holy Spirit of God, recorded by Paul, in the form of thirteen letters. The content is rich. It is beyond the scope of this study to delve into each letter. However, there are select statements in the letters that may bring clarity to the consideration before us; these will be highlighted. Remember that the entirety of Paul's thirteen epistles is holy Scripture. These letters are the inspired revelation of God, as Paul would declare to Timothy, "All Scripture is God breathed" (2 Tim. 3:16).

The letter to the Romans was Paul's most developed letter in regard to soteriology, with emphasis on the righteousness of God. In this epistle, Paul quoted freely from OT texts. The conclusion of the letter is instructive to us:

> Now to him who is able to strengthen you according to my gospel and the preaching of Jesus Christ, according to the revelation of the mystery that was kept secret for long ages but has now been disclosed and through the prophetic writings has been made known to all nations, according to the command of the eternal God, to bring about the obedience of faith—to the only wise God be glory forevermore through Jesus Christ! Amen. (Rom. 16:25–27)

Paul's letters to the Corinthian Church emphasize the wisdom of God. In 1 Corinthians 2, Paul spoke of the work of the Spirit, who had made clear what was hidden in the past (see vv. 7–16). This may not have referred to new revelation but rather to the work of the Holy Spirit in regard to illumination of the OT text. However, as

Paul wrote of marriage in chapter 7, he acknowledged what God had said in the past but also was speaking new revelation.

> To the married I give this charge (not I but the Lord). (1 Cor. 7:10)

> To the rest I say (I, not the Lord). (1 Cor. 7:12)

Paul was not making a distinction between what he was writing and what was already regarded as Scripture. Rather, he was placing his letters on the same level as revelation from God, because it was revelation from God! Later, in verses 25 ff., Paul wrote, "I have no command from the Lord, but I give my judgment as one who by the Lord's mercy is trustworthy."

In chapter 11, Paul spoke of the bread and the cup and declared in verse 23, "For I received from the Lord what I also delivered unto you, that the Lord Jesus on the night when he was betrayed, took bread." At the time of the writing of this epistle, it is unlikely that any of the Gospels had been recorded. Paul was saying that the Lord Himself gave him this revelation. How it came to him, we are not told. In regard to spiritual gifts in chapters 12–14, Paul dealt with prophecy, but it appears to be more of the proclamation of the existing Word of God than a receiving of new revelation from God. The argument could be made that the NT gift of prophecy was essentially preaching. If that is true, then much of the claimed support for extra-biblical revelation is weakened. If NT prophecy was revelatory, we must remember that the canon was still in process.[11] There appears to be a difference between the office of prophet, as in Ephesians 4, and the gift of prophecy as described in 1 Corinthians 12 and 14. We will explore that a bit more later.

In 2 Corinthians, we find Paul in a dilemma regarding a visit to Corinth. All of this was directed providentially by a sovereign God

---

[11.] Joel R. Beeke and Paul M. Smalley, *Reformed Systematic Theology, Volume 1: Revelation and God* (Wheaton, IL: Crossway, 2019), 433–457. This chapter, "The Cessation of Special Revelation, Part 2," is an excellent summary.

rather than by direct revelation from God. Note also in 2 Corinthians 2:12 that a door was open to Paul at Troas to preach the Gospel, but concern for Titus led Paul to leave Troas and head to Macedonia. In 2 Corinthians 12, Paul wrote of the vision he received from God of "the third heaven...caught up into Paradise." Even though the experience was personal, Paul was unsure if the vision was in or out of the body (v. 3). It is instructive how reluctant Paul was to share this vision with others and that fourteen years had passed before he did so.

Paul's letter to the Galatians opened with his astonishment regarding the church's departure from the Gospel. As Paul made his case to the Galatians, he shared some information found nowhere else regarding his salvation and ministry training.

> For I would have you know, brothers, that the gospel that was preached by me is not man's gospel. For I did not receive it from any man, nor was I taught it, but I received it through a revelation of Jesus Christ... But when he who had set me apart before I was born, and who called me by his grace, was pleased to reveal his Son to me, in order that I might preach him among the Gentiles, I did not immediately consult with anyone; nor did I go up to Jerusalem to those who were apostles before me, but I went away into Arabia, and returned again to Damascus. (Gal. 1:11–12, 15–17)

In Paul's letter to the Ephesians, he spoke of the mystery of God's grace related to God bringing the Jews and the Gentiles into one body in Christ, as having come to him by revelation.

> For this reason, I, Paul, a prisoner of Christ Jesus on behalf of you Gentiles—assuming that you have heard of the stewardship of God's grace that was given to me for you, how the mystery was

made known to me by revelation, as I have written briefly. When you read this, you can perceive my insight into the mystery of Christ, which was not made known to the sons of men in other generations as it has now been revealed to his holy apostles and prophets by the Spirit. This mystery is that the Gentiles are fellow heirs, members of the same body, and partakers of the promise in Christ Jesus through the gospel. (Eph. 3:1–6)

Three passages in Ephesians are significant in our discussion:

So then you are no longer strangers and aliens, but you are fellow citizens with the saints and members of the household of God, built on the foundation of the apostles and prophets, Christ Jesus himself being the cornerstone. (2:19–20)

When you read this, you can perceive my insight into the mystery of Christ, which was not made known to the sons of men in other generations as it has now been revealed to his holy apostles and prophets by the Spirit. (3:4–5)

And he gave the apostles, the prophets, the evangelists, the shepherds and teachers, to equip the saints for the work of ministry, for building up the body of Christ. (4:11)

Determining the identity of "prophets" in these three passages has proven to be a challenge. Are these OT prophets or NT prophets, or is Paul speaking of apostles and prophets as one group and not two groups, much like many interpret "shepherds and teachers" (4:11), as one and not two distinct groups of the gifted men that God has given to His church? This option is argued by Wayne Grudem,[12] but apostles and prophets were two distinct categories.

There is no direct reference to any immediate revelation from God in regard to Paul's letter to the Philippians. The same could be said of Paul's letter to the Colossians. In his letters to the Thessalonians, Paul spoke of his anxiety concerning them as he waited for news from Timothy about the genuineness of their faith. Timothy brought positive news for which Paul was greatly encouraged, but Paul did not know until Timothy arrived. There are things in the Thessalonian letters as well as Paul's other letters that were not recorded elsewhere in Scripture, but there was no statement that they were given specifically from God by direct revelation. As Paul wrote, he was being carried along by the Holy Spirit. Philemon may be one of the more intriguing epistles. It was a brief letter written to an individual, quite possibly the host of a house church, concerning a runaway slave who had become a believer. The slave was being sent back to his owner with this letter and probably another letter as well. There was no reference to revelation in this epistle.

Paul's letters to his coworkers, Timothy and Titus, share instruction concerning the establishment of the leadership in the church as well as personal instructions to these two men. Paul's second letter to Timothy, his final letter, provides us with the clearest explanation of the origin of Scripture, as well as its impact on people who would hear it.

> But as for you, continue in what you have learned and have firmly believed, knowing from whom you learned it and how from childhood you have been acquainted with the sacred writings, which are able to make you wise for salvation through faith in Christ Jesus. All Scripture is breathed out by God and profitable for teaching, for reproof, for correction, and for training in righteousness,

---

12. Grudem, p. 46.

that the man of God may be complete, equipped
for every good work. (2 Tim. 3:16–17)

Though the Scripture was recorded by human beings, it was breathed out by God. The originator of all Scripture is God.

Unlike the other NT books, the Epistle to the Hebrews is apologetic, intentionally setting out to prove the superiority of the Lord Jesus Christ over the OT Jewish system.

The unknown author constantly appealed to the OT Scriptures as well as to the historical record of the life, death, and resurrection of Jesus. It is precisely from the first three verses of this epistle that we have developed the thesis for this study. The former focus was on the OT prophets and their revelation. The present focus is on the Lord Jesus Christ, which has come to us via the writings of the apostles in the persons of Matthew, Mark, Luke, John, Paul, Peter, James, and Jude and perhaps one additional author of this book if not written by one of the above.

Two verses in chapter 4 are intriguing:

> For the word of God is living and active, sharper
> than any two-edged sword, piercing to the divi-
> sion of soul and of spirit, of joints and of marrow,
> and discerning the thoughts and intentions of the
> heart. And no creature is hidden from his sight,
> but all are naked and exposed to the eyes of him
> to whom we must give account. (Heb. 4:12–13)

The Scriptures are living in that God continues to speak through them. The Scriptures, directed by the Holy Spirit, accomplish the things that were mentioned by Paul in 2 Timothy 3:16–17. The Scriptures are not, however, an expanding document that remains open for new additions. Most evangelicals would agree that the canon of Scripture is complete and therefore closed to any supposed new revelation to be added to it.

The remainder of the NT letters is sometimes referred to as the General Epistles. James was written to Jewish believers who were scattered, probably due to persecution. The book is rich in OT background, which would be expected in appealing to Jewish people but clearly written to believers in the Lord Jesus (1:1; 2:1). James had something to say about the application of the Word.

> But be doers of the word, and not hearers only, deceiving yourselves. For if anyone is a hearer of the word and not a doer, he is like a man who looks intently at his natural face in a mirror. For he looks at himself and goes away and at once forgets what he was like. But the one who looks into the perfect law, the law of liberty, and perseveres, being no hearer who forgets but a doer who acts, he will be blessed in his doing. (Jas. 1:22–25)

Peter's letters were also written to those of Jewish heritage, although some would suggest differently based on 2 Peter 1:1. Peter spoke of the Lord Jesus and his life with Jesus during His earthly ministry. There was an emphasis on the unity of the Scripture as God's written revelation.

> Concerning this salvation, the prophets who prophesied about the grace that was to be yours searched and inquired carefully, inquiring what person or time the Spirit of Christ in them was indicating when he predicted the sufferings of Christ and the subsequent glories. It was revealed to them that they were serving not themselves but you, in the things that have now been announced to you through those who preached the good news to you by the Holy Spirit sent from heaven, things into which angels long to look. (1 Pet. 1:10–12)

In Peter's second letter, he wrote,

> And we have the prophetic word more fully con-
> firmed, to which you will do well to pay atten-
> tion as to a lamp shining in a dark place, until
> the day dawns and the morning star rises in your
> hearts, knowing this first of all, that no prophecy
> of Scripture comes from someone's own inter-
> pretation. For no prophecy was ever produced
> by the will of man, but men spoke from God as
> they were carried along by the Holy Spirit. (2 Pet.
> 1:19–21)

We saw this earlier in the Gospels as we considered the transfiguration. Notice also 3:1–2.

> This is now the second letter that I am writing
> to you, beloved. In both of them I am stirring
> up your sincere mind by way of reminder, that
> you should remember the predictions of the holy
> prophets and the commandment of the Lord and
> Savior through your apostles.

Finally, in chapter 3, Peter spoke of the value of Paul's letters,
including them as Scripture.

> And count the patience of our Lord as salvation,
> just as our beloved brother Paul also wrote to
> you according to the wisdom given him, as he
> does in all his letters when he speaks in them of
> these matters. There are some things in them that
> are hard to understand, which the ignorant and
> unstable twist to their own destruction, as they
> do the other Scriptures. (vv. 15–16)

Along with the Gospel that bears his name, the apostle John wrote three epistles that are part of holy Scripture. Among the last books written, John wrote with reference to his life with the Lord Jesus. Note for example, 1:1–4. This letter follows a familiar pattern and familiar themes with his Gospel account of the Lord Jesus. In fact, unlike some of the writers of Scripture, John clearly identified the purpose for writing his Gospel (20:30–31) and his first letter (5:13).

Jude was an earthly brother of the Lord Jesus. The opening of his letter provided a clear illustration of what it was like to be "carried along by the Holy Spirit" (v. 3). Intending to write about "our common salvation," he changed direction to appeal to his readers to "contend for the faith that was once for all delivered to the saints." Similar to 2 Peter 2, Jude wrote of the pretenders who had crept into the church. He built his case on OT examples of God's judgments and reminded his readers that those who would lead others away from the faith would likewise be judged. There is instruction and encouragement as well as a doxology to our "only God and Savior"(Jude 25).

The final book of the NT is the Revelation. It was the completion, the final piece of the canon of Scripture which was started for us, "In the beginning," in the Law of Moses, Genesis 1:1. The unveiling of the Lord Jesus in power and great glory, which had been inferred and prophesied and even predicted by the Lord Jesus Himself during His incarnation, was brought into focus through this vision given to the apostle John.

> The revelation of Jesus Christ, which God gave him to show to his servants the things that must soon take place. He made it known by sending his angel to his servant John, who bore witness to the word of God and to the testimony of Jesus Christ, even to all that he saw. (Rev. 1:1–2)

Verses 9–19 explain the source and experience of the revelation.

> I, John, your brother and partner in the tribula-
> tion and the kingdom and the patient endurance
> that are in Jesus, was on the island called Patmos
> on account of the word of God and the testi-
> mony of Jesus. I was in the Spirit on the Lord's
> day, and I heard behind me a loud voice like a
> trumpet saying, "Write what you see in a book
> and send it to the seven churches, to Ephesus and
> to Smyrna and to Pergamum and to Thyatira and
> to Sardis and to Philadelphia and to Laodicea."
> Then I turned to see the voice that was speaking
> to me, and on turning I saw seven golden lamp-
> stands, and in the midst of the lampstands one
> like a son of man, clothed with a long robe and
> with a golden sash around his chest. The hairs of
> his head were white, like white wool, like snow.
> His eyes were like a flame of fire, his feet were
> like burnished bronze, refined in a furnace, and
> his voice was like the roar of many waters. In his
> right hand he held seven stars, from his mouth
> came a sharp two-edged sword, and his face was
> like the sun shining in full strength. When I saw
> him, I fell at his feet as though dead. But he laid
> his right hand on me, saying, "Fear not, I am
> the first and the last, and the living one. I died,
> and behold I am alive forevermore, and I have
> the keys of Death and Hades. Write therefore
> the things that you have seen, those that are and
> those that are to take place after this."

Throughout the book, we are given the images that John saw, and we hear the commands he was given to obey. In chapters 2 and 3, John was told to write the words of Him who holds the seven stars in His hand, words the Lord was dictating to the apostle to give to the churches. Chapter 4 begins, "After this, I looked and behold a door standing open in heaven…I had heard speaking to me." In chapter 1, John had a vision of the Lord. In chapter 4, he had a vision of heaven. In chapters 5–6, he saw the scroll (the title deed to creation) and then he saw the Lamb, and he watched as the Lamb broke the seals and opened the scroll. John watched as the Lord began to pour out His wrath on those who dwelt on the earth (6–16). Much of the time John was a bystander. He recorded what he saw. At other times he was brought into the drama. In chapter 10, he was about to record what he was seeing when he was told, "Seal up what the seven thunders have said and do not write it down" (10:4). A few verses later John was told to take the scroll (v. 8) and eat it (v. 9). And then he was told, "You must again prophesy about many peoples and nations and languages and kings" (v. 11). John was given a measuring rod and told to measure the temple (11:1–2). John watched as Babylon fell (chapters 17–18). In chapter 19, John heard the angelic chorus of "Hallelujah" and then witnessed a vision of the opening of heaven and the return of the Lord. Revelation 19:13 says, "He is clothed in a robe dipped in blood, and the name by which he is called is The Word of God." John continued to observe as Satan was bound and a kingdom was established. He also watched as Satan was loosed for a season and then suddenly cast into the lake of fire. He saw the creation of a new heaven and a new earth. He heard the words and was told to write those words that were *trustworthy and true* (21:5).

> Write this down…It is done! I am Alpha and Omega, the beginning and the end. To the thirsty I will give from the spring of the water of life without payment. The one who conquers will have this heritage, and I will be his God and he will be my son. But as for the cowardly, the faithless, the detestable, as for murderers, the sexually immoral, sorcerers, idolaters, and all liars, their portion will be in the lake that burns with fire and sulfur, which is the second death. (Rev. 21:5–8).

The book of Revelation speaks of familiar Bible themes such as man's corruptness and God's power, Satan's attempts to overthrow and God's ultimate victories. The book highlights the joys and blessings of the redeemed of all the ages and the horror of the judgment of the condemned for all eternity. What began in Genesis is concluded in Revelation. And what concludes in the canonical book of Revelation appears to be the conclusion of God's revelation to His church until He comes to take His people home. The instruction was to remain in the book (1:3) even as we await the Lord's glorious return (21:20).

It is important to note the final instruction of this final book of the sacred text:

> And he said to me, "Do not seal up the words of the prophecy of this book, for the time is near. Let the evildoer still do evil, and the filthy still be filthy, and the righteous still do right, and the holy still be holy. Behold, I am coming soon, bringing my recompense with me, to repay each one for what he has done. I am the Alpha and the Omega, the first and the last, the beginning and the end." Blessed are those who wash their robes, so that they may have the right to the tree of life and that they may enter the city by the gates. Outside are the dogs and sorcerers and the sexually immoral and murderers and idolaters, and everyone who loves and practices falsehood. "I, Jesus, have sent my angel to testify to you about these things for the churches. I am the root and the descendant of David, the bright morning star." The Spirit and the Bride say, "Come." And let the one who hears say, "Come." And let the one who is thirsty come; let the one who desires take the water of life without price. I warn everyone who hears the words of the prophecy of this book: if anyone adds to them, God will add to

him the plagues described in this book, and if anyone takes away from the words of the book of this prophecy, God will take away his share in the tree of life and in the holy city, which are described in this book. He who testifies to these things says, "Surely I am coming soon." Amen. Come, Lord Jesus! The grace of the Lord Jesus be with all. Amen. (Rev. 22:10–21)

The stern warning from John argues strongly against adding anything to the sacred text—anything! The same could be said about taking anything away. Though some might argue that John was limiting the warning that nothing should be added to or taken away from the book of Revelation, the argument could be made that this warning applies to the entire canon of Scripture. Since this book was the final revelation of God, describing the end of the age and the culmination of God's plan and purpose, it is reasonable to conclude that the warning was not just to be applied to the book of Revelation but to the entire canon. There are several declarations in Scripture that command that nothing be added to the text, such as Deuteronomy 4:2, 5:22, 12:32, 18:18; Numbers 11:25, as well as Revelation 22:18–19. O. Palmer Robertson makes the case that God's revelation would be given in various stages, and as those stages were completed, nothing was to be added to them.[13] Regarding Revelation 22, he makes this observation.

> There is a uniqueness to this "Do not add" found in the last verses of the last chapter of the last book of the Bible. All the previous prohibitions indicated a rounding out of the revelation related to a particular phase of the progress of redemption. At the same time, they were anticipating a future "end" of revelation that would come when

---

[13.] O. Palmer Robertson, *The Final Word* (Carlisle, PA: The Banner of Truth Trust, 1993), 61.

> the goal of redemptive history had arrived...the
> book of Revelation holds a unique position in the
> authoritative revelations from God. Presenting
> Christ as he will be seen again only when he
> returns in glory, its admonition that no one must
> presume to add excludes any and all pretentions
> to further revelations.[14]

What are we to make of the history of God speaking through the pages of Scripture? The OT was mostly recorded by prophets who wrote with absolute authority the words of God. We witnessed that authority as we considered the OT. We heard the warnings of judgment that would come to such prophets who claimed divine authority but spoke something else. As the Son of God began His ministry, the role of the prophet and his authority seems to have changed. The authority seen in the OT prophets of God appears to have been granted to the NT apostles. Wayne Grudem, in his book, *The Gift of Prophecy in the New Testament and Today*, makes a credible argument affirming this conclusion in his second chapter, "The New Testament Apostles." By the NT era, prophets seemed to be the proclaimers of truth already revealed rather than bringing fresh revelation from God. Any claim of "thus says the Lord" would be quotations from the OT text, not new truth. Grudem writes,

> To my knowledge, nowhere in the New Testament
> is there a record of a prophet who is not an apos-
> tle but who spoke with absolute divine author-
> ity attaching to his very words. And we have no
> books in the New Testament written by anyone
> who claims to be a "prophet" but not an apostle
> as well. Moreover, in the first 150 years of the
> church, there is (to my knowledge) no record of
> any divinely authoritative word spoken by these
> prophets. We have no collections of "words of the

---

14. Ibid., 65–66.

prophets at Corinth," or "words of the prophets at Thessalonica" or "words of the prophets at Ephesus," or at Tyre, or at Caesarea, etc. Yet if all these prophets were speaking the very words of God, is it not reasonable to suppose that many of these words would have been recorded and preserved for us as Scripture? If such words were indeed equal to Scripture in authority, then why were they not preserved by early Christians? And why is there no indication that any churches *tried* to preserve them?[15]

However the gift of prophecy might be defined, as declared in 1 Corinthians 12–14, it did not appear to carry the same authority as was generally demonstrated and assumed by the OT prophets, nor does it appear to have the same warning of death attached if the prophecy proved untrue, making me wonder if there is to be a distinction between prophets and prophecy. Certainly, the apostles, the eleven, did speak with the authority that was demonstrated by the OT prophets. We saw that, for example, in Paul, as he claimed divine authority for many of the things he was saying. Again, from Grudem,

In our daily lives, it is the words of Scripture alone that must have first place in our hearts and our minds. We must read them, believe them, memorize them, love them and cherish them as the very words of our Creator speaking to us. All other gifts and teachings today are to be subject to the words of Scripture and are to be judged by them. No other gift or teaching or writing should be allowed to compete with them for absolute priority in our lives.[16]

---

[15]. Grudem, 56–57.
[16]. Ibid., 64–65.

We have considered the history of God speaking in the Old and New Testaments. We have noted that primarily the OT text was spoken by prophets through various means, and the NT was the revelation of God, first through the Son and then through those men whom He chose to record this revelation. I think we would affirm that there is little question that what we have in the OT and the NT is the authoritative Word of God. What we have is what God has said! What is less clear, and what remains before us to determine, is what to do with the supposed prophecies and revelations claimed to be from God. Is God still speaking His revelation to His people apart from and/or in addition to His written revelation? Is it legitimate to say, "God spoke to me," when that refers to extra-biblical revelation? And if it is, how are we to receive it in regard to its authority, accuracy, relevance, and application? That is what is before us. We know something about the history of God speaking. Now we need to examine the claims that God continues to speak apart from the Scriptures in light of what we have observed concerning God speaking in the Scriptures.

10

Is God Still Speaking Today?

We have worked our way through the Old and New Testaments noting when and how God spoke throughout recorded biblical history. We have been able to affirm what the author of Hebrews recorded in 1:1–3.

> Long ago, at many times and in many ways, God spoke to our fathers by the prophets, but in these last days he has spoken to us by his Son, whom he appointed the heir of all things, through whom also he created the world. He is the radiance of the glory of God and the exact imprint of his nature, and he upholds the universe by the word of his power.

The phrase, "In these last days," seems to describe the first century from the time of Jesus's incarnation through the completion of the NT canon, about AD 100. The question remains, "Is God continuing to speak, and if so, how?"

Based on what has been discovered in the Scripture, it appears to me that God's revelation is complete, but He continues to speak through the written text. Generally, that is not disputed among evangelicals. What I am arguing, based on the Old and New Testament record, is that God speaks *exclusively* through the Scriptures. He has revealed all He is going to reveal. There is no new revelation from God being given today. The Bible is not just the recorded history of

His revelation. It is the living and active Word of God (Heb. 4:12). When we open to any page in the Bible and read, what we read is God speaking to us. But is this the only way He has chosen to speak?

The question we desire to answer involves additional revelation. If God is speaking to us today apart from and in addition to what is recorded in the Bible, is that to be considered new revelation? If we believe He is speaking in this way, how do we know for certain, and if He is, what do we make of such revelation? Is the quality of this revelation equal to the Bible? Is this revelation inerrant? Is what He is saying to us always true and always be acted upon? Does this revelation contain the same level of authority as Scripture? Should this revelation be heard by a wider audience than just the individual or individuals who received it? If the revelation proves less than accurate, is it still possible that at least parts of it came from God, requiring us to accept the task to discern the wheat from the chaff, the true from the false? When people say, "God spoke to me," if that claim of divine revelation is equal in authority and value to the sacred text, what are we to do with it? If it is not equal in authority and value, the same question applies, but we must further ask, if it is not equal in authority and value as the sacred text, how is that coming from God?

The Scripture speaks of being led by the Spirit. When God leads in whatever way, is that also God "speaking" in the sense of imparting revelatory information? When we have a dream, could that be God speaking? How do we know? Can we be sure? Is God continuing to reveal Himself to certain segments of the world through revelatory dreams such as to the Muslim world, in order to convince them of the deity of Jesus? Many missionaries claim such to be the case. Is there any support for this found in the canonical Scriptures? What are we to make of the gift of prophecy that we find in 1 Corinthians 12–14? Are the "prophets" among the "gifted men" still being given to the church as described in Ephesians 4? If so, are these prophets receiving new revelation from God? We hear of people being called into ministry. How does that call come? Does God speak to certain individuals giving personal revelation to be directed to other individuals or groups? In other words, is God telling you to tell me something? And if you tell me, is it possible for me to be sure this message is from God? These and other questions are before us. Up front, I will explain my understanding and then make the effort to support the position with God's written revelation. In the process, hopefully most, if not all of the questions above, will be addressed with a credible answer.

Let's begin with my conclusion that was reached on the basis of the survey of the Bible that God has indeed completed His revelatory work with the completion of the Old and New Testaments. The Bible reveals something about eternity past when only God existed and makes known to us God's creative work in Genesis 1 and 2 and continues that revelation through the end of the age when God will reconcile all things to Himself. Genesis through Revelation covers every time period to be experienced from eternity past into eternity future. Everything that has ever happened or will happen is contained within these perimeters. For us, the Scriptures are declared to be sufficient for life and godliness:

> His divine power has granted to us all things that
> pertain to life and godliness, through the knowl-
> edge of him who called us to his own glory and
> excellence. (2 Pet. 1:3)

God has revealed Himself and His plan for the ages. There is nothing more that we need in order to live and please God than what has been revealed by God and recorded in the Scriptures. In other words, if God reveals nothing more than what we have in the Scriptures, according to the revelation given to the apostle Peter, we will not lack vital information that we need in order to obey and please Him.

God is certainly able to do anything He desires to do that is consistent with His will and purpose. He is therefore able to speak to any or all of us at any time and in whatever way He chooses. The issue is not His ability but His plan and purpose. Does He choose to do so? He did speak in various ways in the OT, and those words were recorded. But even in the OT, He chose mostly to speak to and through the prophets. Most individuals never heard the voice of God. Most never received a personal message directly from God. Most never received a divine revelatory vision. There were extended periods of time when God did not speak at all to anyone apart from what was recorded. When He did speak, His words were directed mostly to a few specific people, the prophets. When we open the pages of the NT, we are introduced to God Himself in the person of the Lord Jesus Christ. God in flesh spoke to many, to thousands, but most did not know that Jesus was God, and many denied any possibility that He was God, and in the end, most rejected Him as God. After Jesus's death and resurrection and ascension, God chose to speak to men, not so much to the prophets as in the OT but mostly to and through His chosen and appointed apostles. His words, given through them, were recorded in the pages of the NT for all to read. There is no clear evidence in the Scripture, OT or NT, that random individual believers were being given messages from God. He chose rather to speak through the words that were already recorded in the OT and through the words that were given to the apostles by the Spirit and recorded by them as God's Word in the NT.

Once the canon of Scripture was recognized and accepted by those who believed, it was recognized as the authoritative Word of God. There were debates as to the interpretation of various passages in the Bible, but the Bible was generally, universally accepted as the Word of God. It was authentic and thus authoritative. As a written document, everyone who had access to the Bible had access to a speaking God. His words were not for a select few. The question surrounding the Bible was not, "Is this the word of God?" Rather, the question was, "What does it mean?" Extra-biblical "revelation" carries a significant amount of uncertainty in regard to its authenticity even by those who believe that what they received was from God. They think it was from God, but they are just not certain.

It is important to affirm that God is not silent even though His revelatory work has been completed. The Old Testament prophets and the New Testament apostles often quoted what God had already revealed, and that was presented as God speaking. We saw that as we worked our way through the Bible. When we quote from the Bible to support an argument or prove a point, we are making the case that this is what God is saying on the matter, not just what He said but what He continues to say. What God has said is what God says. The Bible is more than a history text. We are not just reading the stories of the past. As we read, God is speaking the stories to us, as it were. The Bible is His word to us even if the context of what we are hearing or reading is not directly for us. To charge those who hold the position that God speaks alone through His Word to mean that God is silent and no longer speaks is a false charge. The view is not that God is silent but that God has spoken by His Son through His Word and that written Word still speaks. What we have in the Word is complete. It is not new; it is timeless.

The issue at hand is revelation. Many would argue that God continues to reveal Himself and His directives to individuals today. These may include visions and/or dreams of what should be said or done by the one receiving them. These may be inner promptings to pray for someone or to go visit someone or to give something to someone, etc. These may include being awakened in the middle of the night with a strong urge to warn someone or help someone. Some people claim to hear voices or see angels or even see and speak with Jesus Himself. There are dozens of claims and not a few books written describing those who have traveled to heaven and back. Are these revelations from God, thus God speaking through various means to move us to respond? Regardless of how these things might be labeled, they are significantly different than the revelation of Scripture.

I would argue that it is probable that revelation and illumination have been confused.

As the author of Hebrews spoke of God's revelatory work, he was referring to the Scriptures, the OT that had been completed and the NT that was in process even as the author recorded his epistle. Once the NT canon was complete with the final words recorded by John in the Revelation, nothing was to be added to the sacred text. It was enough; it was all that was needed. It was a finished product. We often speak of God revealing something to us. We even speak that way regarding the Scriptures: "I was reading the Bible and God revealed some things I had never seen before." What was discovered was not new revelation. It had been there since the document was written. What actually happened was the reader saw something that before had not been noticed. The meaning of the text was illuminated, as it were, by the Holy Spirit of God. Illumination is not revelation. We need to be more precise in our expressions or at least clarify what we mean. Lack of precision can lead to confusion, and confusion can lead to an errant theology and practice.

In John 16, Jesus was teaching His disciples about the work of the Spirit. For the apostles, future revelation was to be given to them.

> I still have many things to say to you, but you cannot bear them now. When the Spirit of truth comes, he will guide you into all the truth, for he will not speak on his own authority, but whatever he hears he will speak, and he will declare to you the things that are to come. He will glorify me, for he will take what is mine and declare it to you. All that the Father has is mine; therefore I said that he will take what is mine and declare it to you. (John 16:12–15)

There were many things that Jesus had not taught His apostles, including some of the things which were to come. Many of those things would be revealed to John. But there was also a ministry of illumination where the Spirit would cause them to remember what Jesus had said:

> But the Helper, the Holy Spirit, whom the Father will send in my name, he will teach you all things and bring to your remembrance all that I have said to you. (John 14:26)

Remembering what was said is not receiving new revelation. We often use the term *revealed* when it would be more precise to use a different term. *Revealed* is a convenient word, but it might be misleading.

Is the Holy Spirit continuing to grant new revelation, or is His work one of bringing to remembrance what we have read and heard from the Scriptures? I would argue that claims of new revelation from God may in actuality be the illuminating work of the Spirit who is bringing to mind the Word that had been hidden in our hearts and minds, maybe for a long time. Various promptings and impressions to respond to various people and situations are formulated by the Holy Spirit using our exposure to the Word, to guide and direct us by way of illumination into areas of obedience to the Word. These are not revelations from God, but they may be God guiding us by His providential hand using His written Word. Pastor and author Gary Gilley wrote about impression:

> The source of our impressions, being subjective feelings, is impossible to identify. Surely we realize that unbelievers have impressions too; where do they come from? Trying to determine the source of impressions is futile, but most impressions come from our own thoughts. We see a person who needs Christ; we know the power and glory of the gospel; we long to tell others about the truth. What would be so strange about feeling an urge to tell folks about the Lord? Because we are impressed to share the gospel or anything else does not mean we have received extra-biblical communication from God. Impressions are impressions.[17]

One of the challenging issues before us is to understand the ministry of the prophets in the New Testament and the meaning of the gift of prophecy as described by Paul in 1 Corinthians 12–14. We have already observed that the NT prophets appeared less involved than the OT prophets in regard to revelation. Revelation from God following the ascension of Jesus came primarily through the apos-

---

[17.] Gary E. Gilley, *Is That You, Lord?* (Webster, NY: Evangelical Press, 2007), 65.

tles, not the NT prophets. The NT was revealed generally to and through the apostles, though Mark, Luke, James, and Jude were not apostles in the sense of the eleven and of Paul. Mark's Gospel source was certainly Peter. Luke's Gospel was written from the eye witness accounts of the apostles, and Luke recorded Acts as a companion of Paul. James is referred to as an apostle in Galatians 1:19, but he was not one of the twelve. Jesus did appear to James following His resurrection (1 Cor. 15:7), and his status was as the leader of the church of Jerusalem. Jude was an earthly brother of Jesus and of James, but he was not specifically referred to as an apostle. But the title of prophet could have correctly been applied to each of these men who were given revelation from God.

What little we saw in regard to the prophets in the book of Acts may suggest and support a different role from what we witnessed in the OT. For example, we were introduced to the prophet Agabus in Acts 11.

> Now in these days prophets came down from Jerusalem to Antioch. And one of them named Agabus stood up and foretold by the Spirit that there would be a great famine over all the world (this took place in the days of Claudius). So the disciples determined, every one according to his ability, to send relief to the brothers living in Judea. And they did so, sending it to the elders by the hand of Barnabas and Saul. (Acts 11:27–30)

Agabus appeared again in Acts 21:

> While we were staying for many days, a prophet named Agabus came down from Judea. And coming to us, he took Paul's belt and bound his own feet and hands and said, "Thus says the Holy Spirit, 'This is how the Jews at Jerusalem will bind the man who owns this belt and deliver him into the hands of the Gentiles.'" (vv. 10–11)

Agabus sounds much like an OT prophet. His "Thus says the Holy Spirit" is similar to the phrase, "Thus says the Lord," which we saw often in the OT. It has been charged by some that what actually happened to Paul was different than what the prophet had predicted in Acts 21. Wayne Grudem writes,

> The events of the narrative itself do not coincide with the kind of accuracy which the Old Testament requires for those who speak God's words. In fact, by Old Testament standards, Agabus would have been condemned as a false prophet, because in Acts 21:27–35 neither of his predictions are fulfilled.[18]

In regard to the supposed mistakes in the details of Agabus's prophecy, D. A. Carson wrote, "I can think of no reported Old Testament prophet whose prophecies are so wrong on the details."[19]

Is that a fair criticism? The disciples decided to act based on Agabus's prophecy of the coming famine by sending Paul and Barnabas to Jerusalem (Acts 11). Acts 11:27 suggests that the ministry of the prophets continued to function, but a transition was clearly happening in regard to the revelation of Scripture. One might argue the specifics in the fulfillment of the prophesy in Acts 21, as does Grudem and Carson, but Agabus was not wrong that Paul would run into trouble in Jerusalem.

Grudem and others use the example of Agabus to define the prophets and the gift of prophecy in 1 Corinthians 12–14. The case is made that though what these prophets received was revelation from God, the degree of accuracy in detail and fulfillment was not required as was true for OT prophets. In other words, these were revelations from God but carried less authority than the revelation given to the OT prophets and the NT apostles. This conveniently

---

18. Grudem, 96.
19. D. A. Carson, *Showing the Spirit: A Theological Exposition of 1 Corinthians 12–14* (Grand Rapids, MI: Baker Academic, 1987), 98.

allows for continued speaking of new revelation without the necessity of the same level of authority and accuracy and timeless universal acceptance. In other words, such revelation was not to be added to the completed canon of Scripture, but it provides an explanation for God to continue speaking revelatory messages to His people, though what these individuals were saying may or may not have been exactly "thus says the Lord." In the case of Agabus and a few others, could it be possible that they were prophets similar to those in the OT, even though God was primarily speaking through the apostles? Is it appropriate to connect the prophet in Acts 11 and 21 to the gift of prophecy in 1 Corinthians 12–14? To use Agabus as a proof text to justify current revelation as a mixture of God's words and our ideas seems to me a stretch.

In regard to the gift of prophecy in 1 Corinthians 12–14, what if it was actually the gift of preaching, proclaiming the Word of God? We who preach are to preach the Word. We quote the Scripture and interpret the Scripture and make applications from the Scripture, calling people to obey the Scripture. Sometimes we miss the meaning of the text. We fail to interpret correctly. We are not receiving new revelation from God but rather are sharing our understanding of God's revelation as has been given and recorded. Every preacher knows that if we were held to the standards of the OT prophets, we would all have been put to death! If the NT gift of prophecy is actually the gift of preaching, that would end the challenges of what to do with these less-than-authoritative revelations from God. Is there any merit to the idea that the gift of preaching is the equivalent to the NT gift of prophecy? Grudem makes a hardline distinction between preaching and teaching and prophecy.

> Rather, a prophecy must be the report of a spontaneous revelation from the Holy Spirit. So, the distinction in quite clear: if a message is the result of conscious reflection on the text of Scripture, containing interpretation of the text and application to life, then it is (in New Testament terms) a "teaching." But if a message is the report of

something God brings suddenly to mind, then it is "prophecy." And, of course, even prepared teachings can be interrupted by unplanned additional material which the Bible teacher suddenly felt God was bringing to his mind—in that case, it would be a "teaching" with some prophecy mixed in.[20]

It seems to me that Grudem and others are on the one hand making a huge distinction in prophets and prophecy in the OT and prophets and prophecy in the NT, which has some support, but then applying the OT prophet model to the NT passages when it fits the point to be made. When Grudem said,

If a message is the result of conscious reflection on the text of Scripture, containing interpretation of the text and application to life, then it is (in New Testament terms) a "teaching." But if a message is the report of something God brings suddenly to mind, then it is "prophecy,"[21]

he is declaring that prophecy cannot be preaching or teaching because prophecy is unattached from the explanation and application of Scripture. The apostle Paul may not have agreed with that assessment, as he writes in 1 Corinthians 14:3, "The one who prophesies speaks to people for their upbuilding and encouragement and consolation." That rather sounds like interpretation and application which happens in preaching and teaching. There are many times in preaching when something will come to mind that is not in the notes or manuscript, which seems at the moment to fit and so is inserted into the sermon. Sometimes that proves to be a valuable addition; sometimes it is a distraction, which, realized later, should not have been included. It could even prove to be disastrous! To call what

---

20. Grudem, 142–143.
21. Ibid., 143.

pops into one's mind prophecy seems to be a stretch. Once again, in the best-case scenario, that probably should be seen as the work of the Spirit in illumination. Sometimes, it is just something that was stored in our brain that came to mind and must be instantaneously evaluated whether or not there is worth in verbalizing it. That is a frequent occurrence for preachers, but is it revelation from God? Is it prophecy?

Grudem makes a distinction between preaching and prophecy, and in that distinction makes his case for continued revelation.

> Prophecy, not only in 1 Corinthians but in the entire New Testament, has two distinct features. First, it must be based on "a revelation." If there is no revelation, there is no prophecy. Second, it must include a public proclamation. The mere reception of a revelation does not constitute a prophecy until it is publicly proclaimed.[22]
>
> Because of this revelation, the prophet would be able to speak to the specific needs of the moment when the congregation assembled. Whereas the teacher or preacher would only be able to obtain information about the specific spiritual concerns of the people from observation or conversation, the prophet would have in addition the ability to know about specific needs through revelation. In many cases the things revealed might include the secrets of people's hearts (cf. 1 Cor. 14:25), their worries or fears (which need appropriate words of comfort and encouragement), or their refusal or hesitancy to do God's will (which need appropriate words of exhortation).[23]

[22.] Ibid., 146.
[23.] Ibid., 152.

Perhaps this would be true if that were God's plan and purpose to give specific new revelation to His people, but does that not take away from the significance of the written revelation of God? Practically speaking, if personal, specific, fresh revelation from God is available to us about our specific needs and concerns, worries, and fears, why is the written Word necessary? Why study and search for answers and direction and wisdom in the Scriptures when those things can be given immediately and specifically? Though the Word itself claims to be all we need and that it is profitable for us, profitability and sufficiency are exchanged for an immediate, fresh, personal word from God!

John MacArthur, in his commentary on 1 Corinthians, says about the gift of prophecy,

> A prophet of God, therefore, is simply one who speaks forth God's Word, and prophecy is the proclaiming of that Word. The gift of prophecy is the Spirit-given and Spirit-empowered ability to proclaim the Word effectively. Since the completion of Scripture, prophecy has no longer been the means of new revelation, but has only proclaimed what has already been revealed in Scripture. The simplest and clearest definition of this function is given by Paul in 1 Corinthians 14:3, "But one who prophesies speaks to men for edification and exhortation and consolation."[24]

The prophets who were preaching the Word were not giving new revelation but were explaining the Word as it was revealed and recorded. Preachers make mistakes. They sometimes misunderstand the Scripture; they say things that prove not to be correct. If these

---

[24] John MacArthur, *The MacArthur New Testament Commentary First Corinthians* (Chicago: Moody Press, 1984), 303.

"prophets" are offering revelation, then what are we to do with words from God that are inaccurate? Wayne Grudem wrote,

> Do those in the charismatic movement today understand prophecy to have a lesser authority? Though some will speak of prophecy as being the "word of God" for today, there is almost uniform testimony from all sections of the charismatic movement that prophecy is imperfect and impure and will contain elements which are not to be obeyed or trusted. The Anglican charismatic leaders Dennis and Rita Bennett write, "We are not expected to accept every word spoken through the gifts of utterance…but we are only to accept what is quickened to us by the Holy Spirit and is in agreement with the Bible… one manifestation may be 75% God, but 25% the person's own thoughts. We must discern between the two."[25]

Grudem is okay with a mixed message. God's message is in there but so are other things not from God. We have to sort it out, discerning truth from error, God's revelation from human wisdom. How can we be sure we get it right? It must be admitted that we might not interpret the Scripture correctly, but we are starting with the truth. We are not sourced with first determining what is true and what is not before we begin to try to understand the meaning of what is before us.[26]

[25.] Grudem, 110.

[26.] O. Palmer Robertson in chapters 3 and 4 of his book, *The Final Word*, challenges many of the claims made by Grudem. Grudem answers those challenges in a review of Robertson's book. This can be found at http://www.waynegrudem.com/wp-content/uploads/2012/04/Robertson-O-Palmer-response-by-WG.pdf.

Costi Hinn and Anthony Wood wrote of those who use the phrase, "God speaks to me," referring to new forms of prophecy and visions and dreams, "words from the Lord." They write,

> Proponents of this view, who find their chief support in 1 Corinthians 14:29 and 1 Thessalonians 5:20–22, must reassess their position. A simple reading of these passages might suggest Paul is requesting the church "pass judgment" (*diakrino*) on prophecies, telling congregants to discern which are truthful and which erroneous; however, if the unidentified object in each text is not the "prophecy" but the prophet himself then each verse aligns with the larger portion of Scripture and simply teaches that each congregation was to assess whether a person giving a message was true or false (i.e., Deut. 13:1–5; Matt. 7:15–20; 1 John 4:1–6; Rom. 16:17–19). This is a much simpler and more consistent interpretation and fits within the larger teaching of the Scripture that God's written Word is authoritative. We must contend that anytime "God speaks" it is always 100% accurate and not up for debate.[27]

We need to take a step back to consider Paul's use of the word *revelation* in 1 Corinthians 14:30 and other NT passages. Sam Storms, a reformed continuationist, comments,

> "In 1 Corinthians 14:30 Paul describes what appears to be an "'ordinary'" church service where prophetic ministry is encouraged and facilitated. If one person is sharing a prophetic word and a "'revelation'" comes to another who

---

27. Costi W. Hinn and Anthony G. Wood, *Defining Deception* (El Cajon, CA: Southern California Seminary Press, 2018), 125–126.

is seated and silent, the person currently speaking should cease and "'yield the floor'" to the one to whom the revelation just came. Without getting into the specifics of how this works yet, my point is that Paul speaks of prophecy as "'revelation'." All genuine prophetic ministry is based upon or flows from a "'revelation'" from God."[28]

Storms then writes,

> Don't be misled by Paul's use of the word "revelation." Not all revelation is the sort of spontaneous disclosure that he has in view in 1 Corinthians 14:30 or the sort of revelation that was accompanied with inspiration and eventual canonization of biblical texts. The Holy Spirit can reveal something to a Christian in the sense that he can enlighten or illuminate the mind so that we understand more clearly some truths that before was obscure and remote.[29]

He continues,

> But more often than not, I suspect that what they've experienced is the Spirit working to enlighten or illuminate them concerning some truth or ethical principle in Scripture.[30]

Sam Storms is all in for extra-biblical revelation, but he seems to be making concessions here that much of what is received as revelation in his continuationist circles is really illumination. I would argue that today, it always is. When Storms poses the question of how we

---

28. Sam Storms, *Practicing the Power* (Grand Rapids, MI: Zondervan, 2017), 82–83.

29. Ibid., 86.

30. Ibid., 87.

are to recognize the difference between revelation and illumination, he says, "There's no simple answer to that question."[31] Paul does use the word *revelation* in 1 Corinthians 14:30. The question for us, "Is the word revelation sometimes used to describe what would be less than God speaking new revelation?" John MacArthur actually sees this as God speaking new revelation, but he reminds us that this is while the NT was being completed and God was continuing to reveal His Word at that time. The canon was not closed. The scenario MacArthur suggests looks something like this: Prophets were preaching, making proclamation from God's Word. As people were listening and "weighing" what was said, someone had a revelation from God. That new revelation (again, remember the time) would take precedence over the preaching. So the prophet who was teaching and preaching would sit and the one with the revelation would be heard. MacArthur sees prophets who were preaching, giving way to one who had a revelation from God, but this occurred before the completion of the canon. Once the canon was closed, revelation ended. Is that possible?

The word *revelation* is from the Greek word that is used more than forty times in the NT always denoting coming from God. It seems possible that Paul was using this word to describe the work of the Holy Spirit, thus coming from God, not as new revelation of Scripture but rather as illumination of the Scripture that may have been related to the text from which the first prophet was speaking. If the premise of this study is correct, that God gave revelation that would be canonical NT Scripture through the apostles, and once that was complete, no further new revelation from God would be forthcoming, this verse presents a challenge. There is no evidence that the person with the revelation was an apostle. There is also no indication that the revelation received was on par with Scripture. I am inclined to believe that Paul was using the word *revelation* in a generic sense.

---

31. Ibid., 88.

In Ephesians 1:16–19, Paul said,

> I do not cease to give thanks for you, remembering you in my prayers, that the God of our Lord Jesus Christ, the Father of glory, may give you the Spirit of wisdom and of revelation in the knowledge of him, having the eyes of your hearts enlightened, that you may know what is the hope to which he has called you, what are the riches of his glorious inheritance in the saints, and what is the immeasurable greatness of his power toward us who believe, according to the working of his great might.

Note that Paul spoke of the "Spirit of wisdom and of revelation" and seemed to identify the results as enlightenment in verse 18. In Paul's letter to the Philippians, he wrote, "Let those of us who are mature think this way, and if in anything you think otherwise, God will reveal that also to you" (3:15). It seems that some in Philippi had a different perspective than Paul. What God "will reveal" seems more like enlightenment on what Paul had taught rather than to receive new revelation.

While Paul did speak of prophecy and the revelation and the gift of prophecy, I would agree with Joel Beeke and Paul Smalley that with the completion of the NT, those came to an end. Arguing from Ephesians 2:20 that the apostles and prophets were the foundation of the church, they wrote,

> We conclude that the New Testament prophets shared the foundational ministry of the apostles as the bearers of new revelation from God concerning Christ and his people. Paul's teaching on prophets helps to account for the inclusion in the New Testament of books written by people who were not apostles, such as Mark, Luke and Jude, but whose words were inspired by the

Spirit to become part of the Holy Scriptures. It also implies that when the apostles completed their foundational mission and died, the prophets likewise passed from the church. The foundation was laid, the New Testament was written, and now we build on it.[32]

I believe O. Palmer Robertson is correct when he wrote,

All of this evidence points to the formation of a body of truth recognized as having come by revelation from God. This revelational material would provide the divine interpretation necessary for the church to understand properly the redemptive events associated with the coming of Christ into the world. Before any inspired Scriptures of the new covenant had been provided to the church, the revelational gifts of prophecy and tongues were being exercised extensively. Partly as an expression of the fullness of the blessings of God's Spirit as he was poured out in the new covenant era, partly as an experience designed to meet the church's need for revelational understanding of the new day into which it was entering until the new covenant Scriptures could be formed, these gifts of revelation at first were in abundant manifestation in the church. But Paul's stress at the end of his life on the importance of holding fast to the doctrine, the tradition, the faith that had been revealed provides a different picture altogether. A process has been completed, an era has come to an end. The church should not expect that new revelations will continue forever to interpret the significance of the coming of

---

32. Beeke, 441.

Christ into the world. Instead, the body of doctrine received by revelation will become the guide
for the life of the new covenant church.[33]

Moving on now to the issue of evangelism and revelation, a
strong challenge to the premise of this book is the claim made by
many missionaries and former Muslims who are now professing
believers, that it was the revelation of God through dreams that ultimately resulted in their conversion to Christ. What are we to make
of this phenomenon? Claims must be examined in the light of the
canonical Scriptures. The Bible is not silent on God's commission to
proclaim the Gospel to all nations. The pattern of evangelism is to
preach the Gospel. God uses the proclamation of His Word to regen-
erate the hearts of those who hear the Word. That work of regenera-
tion is a work of the Holy Spirit of God. However, we are being told
that in the case of Muslim evangelism, that does not work. God must
reveal Himself personally to Muslims through dreams before they
will embrace Christ.

Dennis McBride, in his article, "An Evaluation of Muslim
Dreams & Visions of Isa (Jesus)," wrote,

> I had no desire to resist or even question what
> God might be doing, but I feared these dreams
> of Isa might be little more than extra-biblical
> psychological or spiritual encounters that could
> supplant God's Word and potentially lead their
> participants away from biblical authority rather
> than into it. And I was greatly concerned to hear
> the supposedly biblical rationale some of my fel-
> low conservative Bible teachers were offering in
> defense of this movement. Some former defend-
> ers of the centrality and sufficiency of God's Word
> in evangelism seemed suddenly to be sacrificing
> that doctrine on the altar of subjective mystical

---

33. Robertson, 77.

encounters. I needed to understand why, and
to evaluate their rationale by God's Word. I also
needed to examine Isa's communication to determine if it was consistent with Christ's communication while He was on earth.[34]

McBride went on to examine and evaluate the phenomenon
and concluded that the dreams and visions lacked biblical authority
and should be regarded as extra-biblical experiences that were not
generated by the Holy Spirit.

According to McBride, arguments for God's use of dreams and
visions for evangelizing Muslims fall into four basic categories. The
first view uses Cornelius in Acts 10 as a biblical example. God would
speak in a dream saying that He loves the recipient of the dream and
wants that recipient to seek Him. After the dream, someone comes
along to identify the one in the dream as Jesus. The second view
makes the claim that the culture of the people in the Eastern parts of
the world is filled with the experience of dreams. God accommodates
their culture and appears to them in a manner to which they can
relate. The third view is similar to the first in the initial dreams, but
the dreams are not the Gospel but bring an awareness of the Gospel
and an encouragement to search out the Gospel. Once these people
are converted, the dreams cease. However, the dreams may reappear if
these people need special encouragement in extreme situations such
as facing torture or the possibility of martyrdom. The fourth view
follows more of the pattern of the conversion of the apostle Paul.

There is reason to suspect that the Jesus of Muslim dreams is not
the same Jesus as revealed in the Scriptures. Basically "Isa" is the messenger claiming to be the God of the Gospel. According to McBride,
Isa not only communicates verses or passages from the Bible, but he

---

34. Dennis McBride, "An Evaluation of Muslim Dreams & Visions of
Isa (Jesus), Part 1" (A two-part, online article printed in the June/
July 2013 edition of *Think on These Things*, Volume 19, Issue 3) 1.

also gives messages of encouragement and comfort and instruction that cannot be found in the Bible. McBride asks the question,

> When Jesus Himself speaks, how can it be any-
> thing *less* than authoritative divine revelation?
> Fact is, far from being non-revelatory, these hun-
> dreds of appearances of Isa suggest a contempo-
> rary period of divine revelation rivaling the New
> Testament era itself.[35]

Many of these dreams have been recorded so they can be exam-ined. While the dreams may offer encouragement, they seem to fail at making known the Gospel. Issues of sin, repentance, forgiveness, righteousness, God's holiness, and justice are routinely absent. If the need for salvation is not clear, what are those responding to Isa's invi-tation actually receiving?

After researching the Muslim dreams and visions, McBride drew this conclusion:

> If Muslims were having dreams about Jesus,
> which resulted in opening their hearts to the gos-
> pel, I'd say, "Praise the Lord," because I believe
> the Holy Spirit can use natural dreams to con-
> vict people of their need for salvation and direct
> them to the gospel if He so chooses. However,
> the reports I'm hearing and reading claim that
> Jesus Himself, in the person of Isa, is appearing
> to Muslims in dreams. I must reject the accuracy
> of those claims…and conclude that such dreams
> and visions lack biblical authority and must there-
> fore be viewed as extra-biblical experiences gen-
> erated from sources other than the Holy Spirit.
> I must also continue to pray that the gospel of
> Jesus Christ, not dreams and visions of Isa, will

---

[35] Ibid., 3.

permeate Muslim communities throughout the
world for the glory of our Lord and the salvation
of many precious souls.[36]

Another issue that surfaces regarding God speaking outside of
Scripture involves the call to ministry. Many pastors who have gone
through the process of ordination have been required to answer a
number of Bible and theology questions to determine if they were
qualified for ministry. One of the questions usually asked involves
the "call to ministry." One ordination council on which I served,
the candidate was struggling to answer this very question about his
call. When the examination was completed and the council con-
vened privately to evaluate what we had heard, one of the members
of the council said something like, "If he has no better sense of a
call to ministry than what he told us, I'm not convinced we should
recommend his ordination." Because the candidate did not provide
sufficient proof of "the Lord told me" or "the Lord led me" or "I just
knew in my heart that God was leading me into ministry," he didn't
qualify regardless of his knowledge of the Scripture and the level of
maturity he had attained and the biblical qualifications he had met.

There is no NT model or requirement for ordination. Neither
is there a clear example of a call to ministry other than maybe the
unique call of the apostle Paul. Yet Paul does provide clear instruction in regard to those who would occupy the office of elder in 1
Timothy 3 and in Titus 1. There was to be a desire on the part of
the candidate, and he was to be able to meet the qualifications given.
Recognition of meeting those qualifications would come from the
other elders who would be considering him.

When the Bible uses the word *call*, it is generally describing the
"call to salvation." In the Gospels, the word *call* is sometimes used in
regard to evangelizing with the Gospel: "many are called, but few are
chosen." In 1 Corinthians 7, Paul wrote, "Each one should remain in

---

[36.] Dennis McBride, "An Evaluation of Muslim Dreams & Visions of
Isa (Jesus), Part 2" (A two-part, online article printed in the August/
September 2013 edition of *Think on These Things*, Volume 19, Issue 4) 7.

the condition in which he was called." The condition of which Paul spoke involved the Jewish rite of circumcision and the institution of slavery. In regard to slavery, his argument was captured in verses 22–24:

> For he who was called in the Lord as a bondser-
> vant is a freedman of the Lord. Likewise, he who
> was free when called is a bondservant of Christ.
> You were bought with a price; do not become
> bondservants of men. So, brothers, in whatever
> condition each was called, there let him remain
> with God.

A Gentile man who was called to salvation did not need to be circumcised. A slave who was called to salvation did not need to seek freedom from his master.

Those who desired the office of elder and met the qualifications did not need to wait for a confirming "word from the Lord." They rather were to continue to be faithful to the Lord in service to Him and watch as He might providentially open opportunity to serve Him in even greater capacity.

God often uses a variety of providential situations and circumstances and people to direct the paths of life for His people. That happened to me. Providentially, I enrolled into a school that trained pastors and missionaries, though I had little interest in either of those vocations. A series of people, a public high school teacher, a college friend, an associate pastor who rode the bus from the school to a distant church and back, always talking to the "preacher boys" who were on the bus, a conversation with a vocational electronics teacher who encouraged me to consider another field of opportunity, convinced that I had no mechanical ability—these and many other people were used by God to direct me into pastoral ministry. There was no voice, no vision, no dream, no warm feelings, but also no doubt that God directed my path and no regret having followed this path. There was, however, confirmation from the Scripture that God had opened the way and given the desire and was working by His Spirit to prepare me to do the work of ministry which He had prepared beforehand. It was not a call but a predetermined plan being worked out in my life by a sovereign God.

There is little pushback today on continued revelation from God. Extra-biblical revelation is assumed and taught in churches and Christian media. *Jesus Calling* (and the sequels to it) are examples of devotional books that have been widely read by the evangelical church.[37] Books such as these are based on impressions and voices, audible and inaudible, that are assumed to be from God. Though generally the revelations are declared to be on a level below Scripture in authority and significance, they are declared to be from God, and they are believed to be immediate, fresh, and significant divine revelations. Regardless of the claim of lesser value to the Scriptures, in practice, the revelations take precedence over Scripture. Most of these revelations are benign with regard to direct contradiction of Scripture. Often that is the argument used to prove authenticity. It goes something like this: "If these revelations are not contrary to Scripture, surely they must be from God." The content of these revelations, however, is added to one's understanding of God's character and what is expected from God. These revelations may skew the recipient's understanding of the meaning of the biblical text. What is read in Scripture will likely be interpreted through the lens of that supposed revelation rather than basing the interpretation on a careful examination of the text of Scripture in its context. Again, in practice, there will likely be less and less dependence on the written revelation of God and more and more emphasis placed on the immediate, personal revelation received. What if these revelations are not from God? Once they are received as genuine and thus authoritative, the recipient is hooked, and wherever those revelations go, consistent with or contrary to the Bible, they will be believed to be from God. Many who accept the concept of God speaking new revelation today

---

[37.] An excellent critical review of the book can be viewed online by pastor and author Gary E. Gilley at his "Think On These Things" website. The book, *Jesus Calling,* was reviewed February 20, 2014.

caution us to be discerning and to compare these revelations with Scripture, but in practice, that is unlikely to happen.

In Sarah Young's book, *Jesus Calling*, she often speaks of the presence of God. God declares in His Word that He is with us. We may "feel" His presence. We may not. But that does not change the truth that if we belong to Him through His saving grace received through the Gospel of His Son, He is with us, and He will never leave us. That's His promise to us. His Spirit indwells us all the time. God has told us the truth in His Word. It's recorded. Every time we read those truths in the sacred text, that is God speaking to us, reminding us that He has not abandoned us or even taken a break from being with us. We do not need a "fresh, new revelation" outside of Scripture to tell us of His presence. Statements like, "Look into My Face and feel the warmth of My Love-Light shining upon you" (p. 278) and "Sit quietly in My Presence, allowing My Light to soak into you and drive out any darkness lodged within you" (p. 294),[38] go well beyond Scripture, adding detail that distorts the truth of what is recorded. What do those phrases even mean? Generally, we "look in His face" when we open the Scripture. The light that drives out the darkness is the application of the Scripture by the Holy Spirit to us. But that is not what the author is suggesting. Instead, the revelations are a call to a mystical relationship with Jesus that the Bible would warn against!

Sitting with pen and paper in hand waiting for divine revelation to be communicated is an open invitation to an active imagination and possibly to a devious enemy. A better use of pen and paper would be to start with an open Bible and write down insights and applications that come to mind as the Scripture is being considered. In so doing, the revelation we have—that is, the Scripture—is certain and authentic, and the Holy Spirit may well shine the light on the text illuminating the meaning for us. We know for certain that the words of Scripture are from God, and we also know that one of the ministries of the Holy Spirit is to shine the light of understanding on Scripture to help us see God and His glory in them. Once again, we

---

[38.] Sarah Young, *Jesus Calling* (Nashville, TN: Thomas Nelson, 2004), 278, 294.

must exercise great care in relation to feelings and emotions. They matter, but they are not the source for revelation.

A final issue I will consider involves our conscience and God speaking. We have a conscience. It has been given to us by God. We have all been stopped in our tracks from doing certain things because our consciences have been awakened. The conscience is not the same as the Holy Spirit; for believers and unbelievers alike have a conscience. We need to take a quick look at the conscience and then determine if there is any connection between conscience and a speaking God.

Conscience could be defined as a capacity to reflect the moral aspects of the image of God. The great difference in how well we reflect the moral aspects of God's image is affected by the capacity we have developed in this area. Consider this from the apostle Paul:

> For when Gentiles, who do not have the law, by nature do what the law requires, they are a law to themselves, even though they do not have the law. They show that the work of the law is written on their hearts, while their conscience also bears witness, and their conflicting thoughts accuse or even excuse them on that day when, according to my gospel, God judges the secrets of men by Christ Jesus. (Rom. 2:14–16)

Though what we do may not be seen or known by anyone, we have a sense that God sees and knows, and what is seen and known is bound to come up at the judgment! The conscience is about right and wrong. For the believer, we may not be able to discern whether it is the Holy Spirit or conscience working in us when what we are challenged to do or not to do is consistent with what we believe to be right or wrong. It is probable that the Holy Spirit works through our conscience bringing conviction and direction. As believers, we have something of a sanctified conscience. We can ignore our conscience, and eventually, we will no longer be sensitive to it.

> Now the Spirit expressly says that in later times some will depart from the faith by devoting themselves to deceitful spirits and teachings of demons, through the insincerity of liars whose consciences are seared. (1 Tim. 4:1–2)

Or we can pile on a bunch of rules to the point that we declare an offended conscience over anything and everything that comes to us from others. John MacArthur writes,

> The conscience is not to be equated with the voice of God or the law of God. It is a human faculty that judges our actions and thoughts by the light of the highest standard we perceive.[39]

How do we respond to our conscience? Essentially, we need to obey it. Paul makes the argument in Romans 14 and 1 Corinthians 8. Here's an example. The leadership in our local church believes that God ordained marriage and marriage is to be for life. The leadership also teaches that God is sovereign. He can change anyone's heart. After all, He changed us. In life, sinners sin. Sometimes they are unfaithful. Sometimes they do evil. Sometimes they are mean and dangerous. Marriages fall apart because of sin. When a marriage dissolves, sometimes those divorced people find new love and remarry. That happens. The Bible speaks clearly on God's intention for marriage to be lifelong, and of His hatred of divorce—but to be fair, He hates all sin. Many churches and church leaders find "loopholes" for remarriage after divorce in Paul's discussion in 1 Corinthians 7. They also find permission in the recognition that God is a God of grace and a God who forgives. The leadership in our local church does not

---

[39.] John MacArthur, *The Vanishing Conscience* (Dallas, TX: Word Publishing, 1994), 37.

officiate weddings involving divorced people. There are many people in the church who have been divorced and who have remarried. There is no stigma or limitation in their attendance and very little limitation in service. It could be asked, "Then why the big deal about not doing weddings involving divorced people?" The answer mostly is a matter of conscience. It goes something like this: We teach that marriage is to be for life. If a couple divorces, the biblical teaching is to pursue reconciliation or remain single, knowing that God is able to work in the hearts of people to bring change and to restore and also to give grace to remain single if reconciliation does not occur. If reconciliation remains a possibility, no matter how remote, then to conduct a wedding for that individual is to end any possible reconciliation. For me to participate in the wedding would be to defile my conscience, and for me, that would be wrong.

Should we always obey our conscience? Paul seems to make the case in Romans 14 and 1 Corinthians 8 that we are to obey our consciences. But what if our consciences are wrong? What if they are oversensitive or seared? Can the conscience ever be reconditioned or changed or instructed? The answer is yes if we belong to the Lord and we gain instruction from the Word that directs us to reconsider how we are responding. Part of Paul's argument involved what was eaten. There was surely a conscience explosion the first time some Jews took a bite of pork. It no doubt took some time before some were able to eat certain foods without guilt. The answer to this was not a voice from heaven giving permission or not. The conscience can be trained by exposure to the truth of the Word of God. But again, it may take some time. Growing up, I was taught that it was sinful to do certain things on the Lord's Day. To do work that could be done on another day of the week was considered an offense worthy of severe discipline from the Lord. Mowing one's grass on Sunday was included in that prohibition! To this day, even if the grass is embarrassingly tall and Sunday is the only day in the immediate future not calling for rain, I can't do it. My conscience screams, "No!" Intellectually and spiritually, I believe it best to set aside the day as a day unto the Lord, but I would not be under judgment if I started the lawnmower. However, conscience still refuses! That's not God telling me not to mow my grass. That is the moral conviction that has developed over a lifetime impacting my understanding of right and wrong. I still don't mow my grass on Sunday, but exposure to the Scripture and maturity in Christ has made me far less sensitive in my conscience (and less judgmental toward others)! John MacArthur, in his book, *The Vanishing Conscience*, wrote,

> The conscience functions like a skylight, not a light bulb. It lets light into the soul; it does not produce its own. Its effectiveness is determined by the amount of pure light we expose it to, and by how clean we keep it. Cover it or put it in total darkness and it ceases to function. That's why the apostle Paul spoke of the importance of a clear conscience (1 Tim. 3:9) and warned against anything that would defile or muddy the conscience (1 Cor. 8:7).[40]

What about my conscience and God speaking? As believers, the Holy Spirit, in conjunction with the Word of God, "supercharges" our consciences. We have an enhanced understanding of right and wrong, of what does or does not glorify God. It is not a result of God speaking to us outside of Scripture, informing us through our conscience. It is the Spirit using the Word to bring our consciences into conformity to the Word of God. This does not involve new revelation, but it does involve illumination of the truth so that we are alerted when we wander close to the edge of that which would be dishonoring to God.[41]

[40.] Ibid., 39.

[41.] For further consideration of the conscience, see *Conscience: What It Is, How to Train It, and Loving Those Who Differ* by Andrew David Naselli and J. D. Crowley, and also see *The Vanishing Conscience* by John MacArthur.

CONCLUSIONS

We have covered significant ground since we began our study together. Based on what we have observed and considered, what legitimate conclusions can we draw? We started with a brief look at Hebrews 1:1–2:

> Long ago, at many times and in many ways, God spoke to our fathers by the prophets, but in these last days he has spoken to us by his Son, whom he appointed the heir of all things, through whom also he created the world.

We noted that God spoke in various ways in the OT, but when His Son came, things were different. Revelation came through Him. We looked at the OT record to try to identify those, "at many times and in many ways" that God spoke to His people. As the author of the epistle to the Hebrews makes clear, we found it to be true that God primarily spoke to and therefore through the OT prophets. The methods God used included personal encounters with God and the angel of the Lord, voices, dreams, visions, Urim and Thummim, etc. The entire record of the OT text is the breathed-out Word of God, mostly recorded by the OT prophets, though what was recorded was guided and guarded by the Holy Spirit resulting in an authoritative, inerrant record of divine revelation.

We noted that there were times of silence when God did not speak. We also noted that God rarely spoke to random individuals. He also rarely spoke of personal matters to those to whom He gave revelation. Passages that are used for support of new revelation were examined in their context to make certain that any application we

might make was not read into the text but could come legitimate-
ly from the text. One text that we specifically considered involved
Elijah at Mt. Horeb and the "still, small voice." This passage cannot
support what is often claimed regarding God speaking today.

Certainly, we could affirm what the author of Hebrews recorded
in 1:1–2 regarding the OT Scriptures. Then we turned to the
Gospels. These are four unique accountings of the life and ministry
of God incarnate, the Lord Jesus Christ. We read the words of Jesus
as recorded by these four human authors, Matthew, Mark, Luke, and
John. No longer was God communicating through prophets. God
Himself was speaking through His Son, who is the exact image of
the Father.

In our studies in the Gospels, we discovered some of the instruction that Jesus gave to His apostles. We learned that they would write
about Jesus, not only recording the events of His life (the Gospels)
but also the record of His working through them after His ascension;
that record included the epistles. Jesus told His apostles (recorded in
John 16:12–15),

> I still have many things to say to you, but you
> cannot bear them now. When the Spirit of truth
> comes, he will guide you into all the truth, for he
> will not speak on his own authority, but whatever
> he hears he will speak, and he will declare to you
> the things that are to come. He will glorify me,
> for he will take what is mine and declare it to
> you. All that the Father has is mine; therefore, I
> said that he will take what is mine and declare it
> to you.

Here was the explanation of how and why the NT epistles were
included in the words of the author of Hebrews: "in these last days
he has spoken to us by his Son." The Son gave His words to the
Spirit, and the Spirit gave those words to the apostles. The apostles,
we learned, now assumed the role similar to the OT prophets. They
were the instruments through whom God gave His revelation to His

people, including us. When Jesus prayed as recorded in John 17, He said,

> As you sent me into the world, so I have sent them into the world. And for their sake I consecrate myself, that they also may be sanctified in truth. I do not ask for these only, but also for those who will believe in me through their word.

Notice that people would believe through "their word." What they would write was the truth to which they were guided. So, in the past, God spoke to us through the prophets as recorded in the pages of the OT. But in these last days, the days of the incarnation and beyond, God spoke to us by His Son directly and by His Son through the instrument of the apostles as they recorded the words of the NT in the first century.

The OT record began in eternity past, and the NT record ends in eternity future, covering the entire work of God in relation to humanity. We know, because of God's revelation, how everything got here, and we know, again through His revelation, how all will come to completion. Though we do not have every detail of God's plan and purpose, we have everything we need for life and godliness until the end of the age.

The apostle John wrote in the final book of the canon of Scripture,

> The Spirit and the Bride say, "Come." And let the one who hears say, "Come." And let the one who is thirsty come; let the one who desires take the water of life without price. I warn everyone who hears the words of the prophecy of this book: if anyone adds to them, God will add to him the plagues described in this book, and if anyone takes away from the words of the book of this prophecy, God will take away his share in the tree of life and in the holy city, which are

> described in this book. He who testifies to these things says, "Surely I am coming soon." Amen. Come, Lord Jesus! The grace of the Lord Jesus be with all. Amen. (Rev. 22:17–21)

When he dropped his quill after writing those words, the revelation of God was complete. It was divinely preserved in a document that all could read or hear. God could have continued to speak, providing additional revelation to His people, but it was not needed. A universal, tested, and authenticated revelation was in the hands of His people to study and contemplate and apply, remembering that what was read in the recorded Word was not only a record of God having spoken but a record of God continuing to speak. What He said as recorded, He says to us now. He is a speaking God, but His speech is within the parameters of His written revelation.

The challenges to this conclusion are many. Some believe that such a viewpoint limits God's ability to communicate His will to us. But generally, God directs through wisdom, a wisdom given to us by Him through His Word and His providence, which is the invisible workings of a sovereign God, not through new revelation. Some look at Paul's words to the Corinthians regarding spiritual gifts and insist that the gift of prophecy would be impossible without new revelation. We concluded that the gift of prophecy may not be what it is assumed as new revelation but perhaps more on the order of preaching than the receiving and proclaiming of something new from God. It is also probable that the gift of prophecy ceased with the completion of the canon of Scripture. Those who advocate new revelation are caught in the challenge to explain the nature of this revelation and are forced to define it as something less than Scripture and something mixed with potential human ideas and errors, leaving the prophet and the hearers of the prophecies to sort out what is from God and what is not, and to determine the value and significance of that which is from God in relation to inerrancy and authority, and then what to do with it once it is received and "verified" as genuine.

Affirming something to be the Word of the Lord when it is not leaves us with a fallible message that bears His name. Granting divine status to anything outside of the Word of God lessens the status and potential authority of the written Word of God. If we must have additional revelation from God, then the message we are communicating is that the written Word is not sufficient, and thus the lack must be made up by these extra-biblical revelations. Those who accept additional revelation are in effect communicating that God has more to say which did not make the first edition!

I was thrilled when I came across an article by John Piper, "The Morning I Heard the Voice of God." Piper spoke of what he heard from God and responded with this:

> Think of it. Marvel at this. Stand in awe of this. The God who keeps watch over the nations—like some people keep watch over cattle or stock markets or construction sites—this God still speaks in the twenty-first century. I heard his very words. He spoke personally to me.
>
> What effect did this have on me? It filled me with a fresh sense of God's reality. It assured me more deeply that he acts in history and in our time. It strengthened my faith that he is for me and cares about me and will use his global power to watch over me. Why else would he come and tell me these things?
>
> It has increased my love for the Bible as God's very word because it was through the Bible that I heard these divine words and through the Bible I have experiences like this almost every day. The very God of the universe speaks on every page into my mind—and your mind. We hear his very words. God himself has multiplied his wondrous deeds and thoughts toward us; none can compare with him! I will proclaim and tell of them, yet they are more than can be told (Psalm 40:5).

And best of all, they are available to all. If you would like to hear the very same words I heard on the couch in northern Minnesota, read Psalm 66:5–7. That is where I heard them. Oh, how precious is the Bible. It is the very word of God.

In reference to an article he had read, he continued,

What's sad is that it really does give the impression that extra-biblical communication with God is surpassingly wonderful and faith-deepening. All the while, the supremely glorious communication of the living God which personally and powerfully and transformingly explodes in the receptive heart through the Bible every day is passed over in silence… I grieve at what is being communicated here. The great need of our time is for people to experience the living reality of God by hearing his word personally and transformingly in Scripture. Something is incredibly wrong when the words we hear outside Scripture are more powerful and more affecting to us than the inspired word of God.[42]

As much as I was glad for what he had said in the article, I was sad that Piper seems to have adopted the same position on extra-biblical revelation as Wayne Grudem. What Piper does here is demonstrate the danger in accepting revelation outside of the written text.

We noted some practical implications and issues that result from the view that God continues to speak outside of His Word. We considered Muslim evangelism and the phenomenon of dreams that speak of Isa (or Jesus) speaking to them, in effect preparing them for the reception of the Gospel. We noted that this is something

---

[42.] John Piper, *The Morning I Heard the Voice of God*, March, 2007.

new in regard to God's written revelation concerning evangelizing the lost—something that is not included in the Scripture. The Bible teaches that it is the Holy Spirit who convicts of sin and regenerates the unbeliever. There is no mention in the written text of Scripture of any dreams or visions to prepare one's heart to believe.

What about hunches or impressions or mystical feelings through which God is communicating something to us? Generally, God leads through His Word and by His providence. When we are impressed to do something that is consistent with what God has already told us, it is probably the Spirit of God illuminating what has already been hidden in our hearts, and through His providence, He is guiding us to accomplish His will. It's not new revelation. It's the illuminating work of the Holy Spirit.

We looked at popular devotional methods such as those included in the book *Jesus Calling* that supposedly help us to learn to hear God's voice. We considered the dangers of practicing the methods suggested such as sitting with a pen and paper waiting for God to say something and then writing it down. We noted that though most who believe in a continuing revelation from God do declare the significance and authority of the Bible, in reality, if God is continuing to speak personal messages to individual believers (and in some cases even unbelievers in some pre-evangelism preparation), the Bible will inevitably fall into disuse. Why search for an answer to a question or try to discern some direction to follow or mine the depths of Scripture for wisdom to make a decision that may be hidden somewhere within a couple thousand-page book when the answer can be received immediately and specifically from God Himself? People like James Ryle would have us believe that the Bible is the infallible record of God's past speaking, but in regard to words for today, God must speak fresh revelation. John MacArthur writes,

> Anyone who is truly convinced that God is speaking fresh words of revelation will inevitably view the later prophecies as somehow more relevant and more personal than the message of Scripture, which is more than two thousand years old.

Inevitably, wherever personal prophecy has been stressed, Scripture has been deemphasized. Two thousand years of church history confirms this to be true.[43]

God's Word is enough for His people. A closed canon speaks to the adequacy of Scripture so that we might be thoroughly equipped, lacking nothing for life and godliness. What we have in the Word of God is authentic and proven. Anything outside of Scripture does not carry the same authenticity. John MacArthur reminds us,

> The quest for additional revelation from God actually denigrates the sufficiency of "the faith which was once for all delivered to the saints" (Jude 3). It implies that God hasn't said enough in the Scriptures. It assumes that we need more truth from God than what we find in His written Word. But as we have repeatedly seen, the Bible itself claims absolute sufficiency to equip us for every good work. If we really embrace that truth, how can we be seeking the voice of God in subjective experiences?[44]

The *Westminster Confession of Faith*, with reference to the sufficiency of Scripture, says,

> The whole counsel of God, concerning all things necessary for His own glory, man's salvation, faith, and life, is either expressly set down in Scripture, or by good and necessary consequence may be deduced from Scripture: unto which nothing at

---

[43.] John MacArthur, *Reckless Faith: When the Church Loses Its Will to Discern* (Wheaton, IL: Crossway Books, 1994), 185–186.

[44.] Ibid., 181.

any time is to be added, whether by new revelations of the Spirit, or traditions of men.[45]

MacArthur writes,

> Does this mean God has stopped speaking? Certainly not, but He speaks today through His all-sufficient Word. Does the Spirit of God move our hearts and impress us with specific duties and callings? Certainly, but He works through the Word of God to do that. Such experiences do not involve new revelation but illumination when the Holy Spirit applies the Word to our hearts and opens our spiritual eyes to the truth. We must guard carefully against allowing our experience and our subjective thoughts and imaginations to eclipse the authority and the certainty of the more sure Word.[46]

Anthony Wood and Costi Hinn, answering frequently asked questions, wrote,

> The Word of God was declared by Christ Himself and propagated by special apostles designated to write it (Heb. 1:1–2; 2:3–4; Matt. 16:15–19; John 14:26; Eph. 2:19–20). So, the church now lives by *sola Scriptura* and to tamper with the central truth invites a host of theological and practical problems. Anything that diverts a Christian's

---

[45]. *Westminster Confession of Faith*, Article VI (Quoted from *Reformed Confessions of the 16th and 17th Centuries in English Translation*, Volume 4, 1600–1693, 235).

[46]. John MacArthur, *Strange Fire* (Nashville, TN: Thomas Nelson, 2013), 117.

attention, joy, memorization, meditation, and reliance away from Scripture must be rejected.[47]

One of my seminary professors, Dr. John C. Whitcomb Jr., would affirm the conclusion, when he wrote,

> The church doesn't need new revelation from heaven today! We already have the completed Bible and the Holy Spirit of God to interpret and apply it! The church doesn't need more apostles to guide her through the troubled waters of this Satan-dominated world. An apostle might fail us as Peter did at Antioch. That is why the Holy Spirit wrote, through Peter himself, that "we have the prophetic word made more sure to which you do well to pay attention as a light shining in a dark place" (2 Peter 1:19). The church doesn't need special powers like those promised to the apostles in Mark 16:17–18, namely, 1) to cast out demons, 2) to speak with new tongues, 3) to pick up serpents, 4) to drink deadly poisons, 5) to heal the sick. The church doesn't need any holy places, healing centers, faith healers, or signs and wonders to appeal to the five senses. What the church needs is a new confrontation with the whole counsel of God, proclaimed in the power of the Holy Spirit with authority and love by men who know their God and who honor His only written revelation. Then and then only may we expect our deepest needs to be supplied and God's purpose for His church to be accomplished in our day.[48]

[47.] Costi W. Hinn and Anthony G. Wood, *Defining Deception* (El Cajon, CA: Southern California Seminary Press, 2018), 126.

[48.] John Whitcomb Jr., "Contemporary Theology Notes" (Grace Theological Seminary classroom syllabus, 1977).

ABOUT THE AUTHOR

Les Martin (M. Div., Grace Theological Seminary; D. Min., Trinity Evangelical Divinity School) has served three churches as pastor-teacher for more than four decades. Most recently he served Lakeview Church in Zion, IL, for thirty-two years. He and his wife, Karen, have four grown children and seven grandchildren.

CPSIA information can be obtained
at www.ICGtesting.com
Printed in the USA
LVHW031017150821
695287LV00001B/24

9 781098 090982